Salvador

DALI

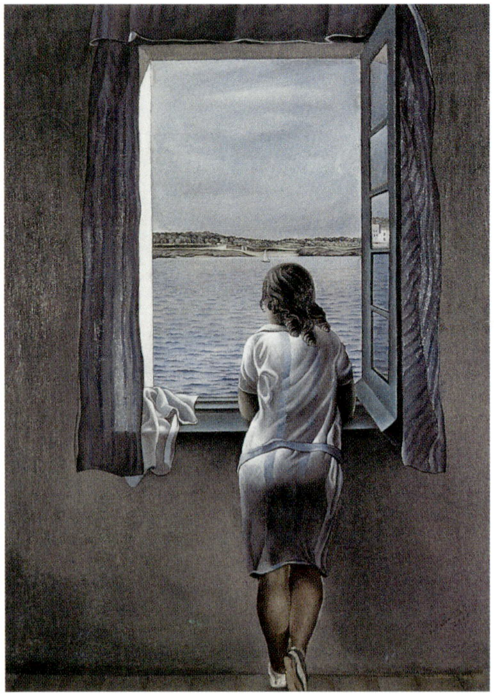

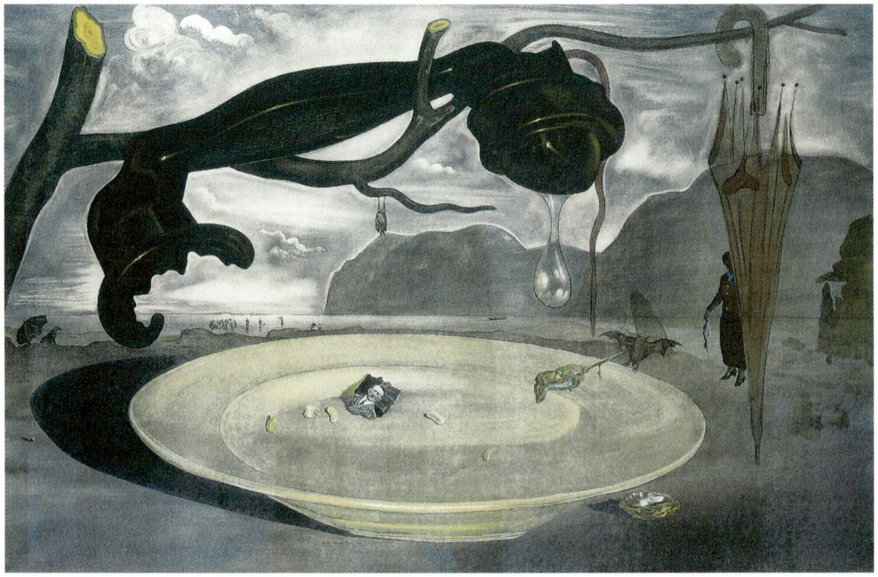

Published in 2003 by Grange Books
an imprint of Grange Books Plc
The Grange Kingsnorth Industrial Estate
Hoo, nr Rochester Kent ME3 9ND
www.Grangebooks.co.uk
ISBN 1-84013-558-1

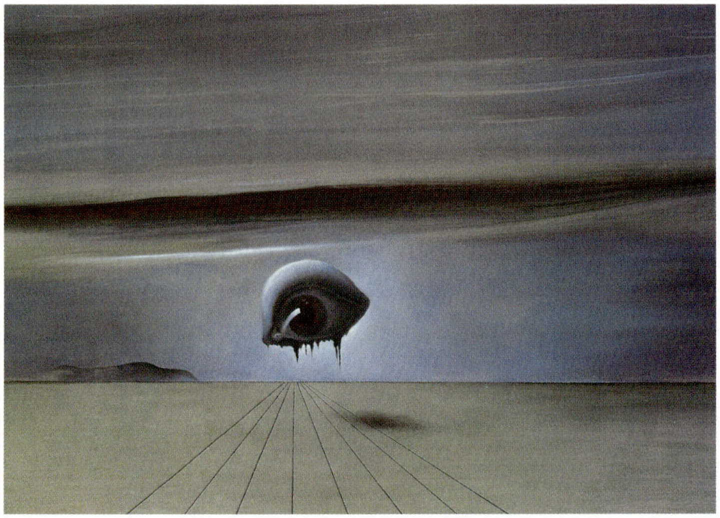

Salvador

DALI

Grange Books

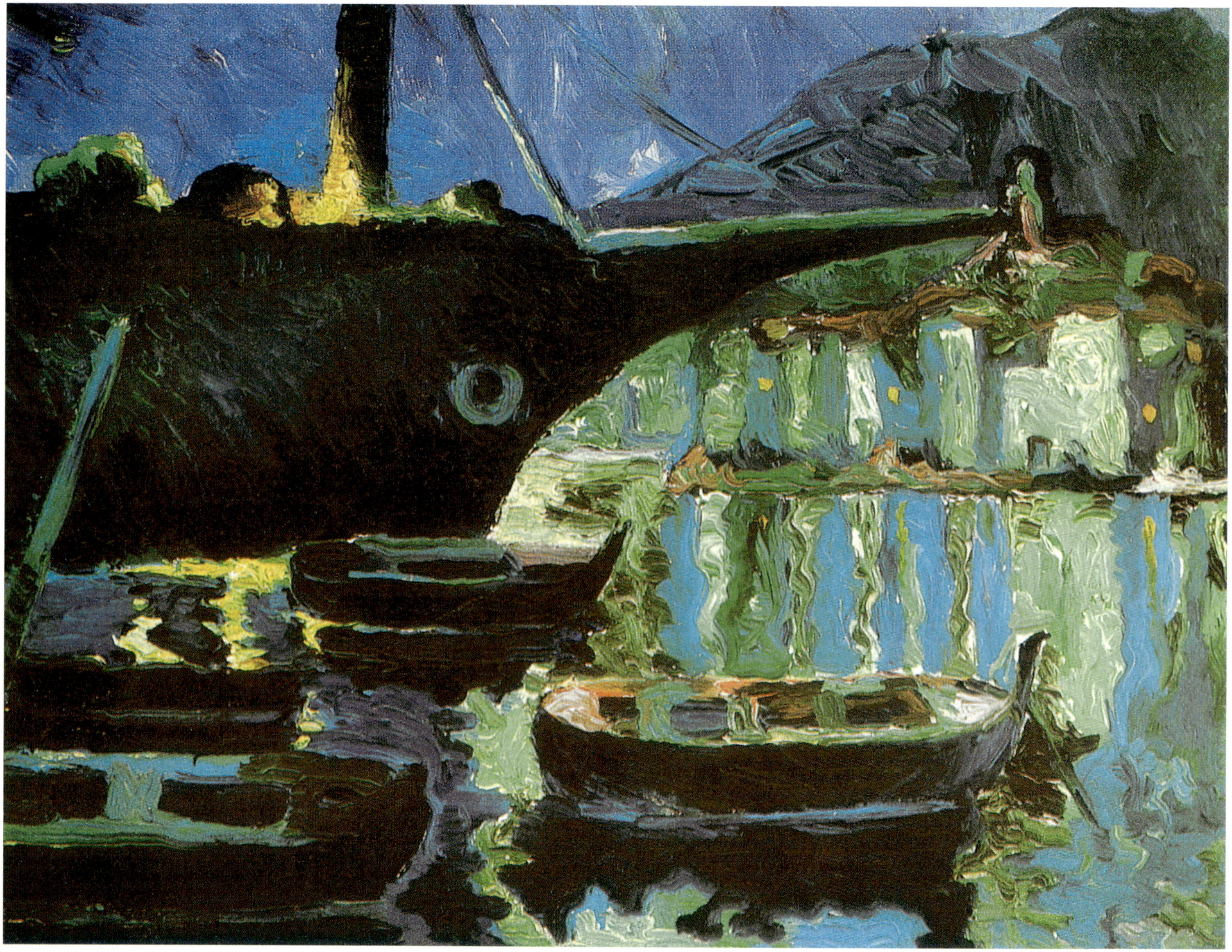

The Public Secret of Salvador Dalí

At the age of 37, Salvador Dalí wrote his autobiography. Titled *The Secret Life of Salvador Dalí*, the Spanish painter portrays his childhood, his student days in Madrid, and the early years of his fame in Paris up to his leaving to go to the USA in 1940. The exactness of his descriptions are doubtful in more than one place. Dates are very often incorrect, and many childhood experiences fit too perfectly into the story of his life. The picture that Dalí drew of himself in 1942, and further developed in the years up to his death in 1989, shows an eccentric person, most at ease when placed in posed settings. Despite this tendency, Dalí often revealed intimate details of his life in front of the camera. This act of self-disclosure, as Dalí explains in his autobiography, is a form of vivisection, a laying bare of the living body carried out in the name of pure narcissism. The more Dalí showed himself in public, the more he concealed himself. His masks became ever larger and ever more magnificent: he referred to himself as "genius" and "god-like". Whoever the person behind Dalí really was, it remains a mystery.

The Years of the King

Childhood and Adolescence in Figueras and Cadaqués

Dalí's memories appear to begin two months before his birth on May 11th, 1904. Recalling this period, he describes the "intra-uterine paradise" defined by "colours of Hell, that are red, orange, yellow and bluish, the colour of flames, of fire; above all it was warm, still, soft, symmetrical, doubled and sticky."[1] His most striking memory of birth, of his expulsion from paradise into the bright, cold world, consists of two eggs in the form of mirrors floating in mid-air, the whites of which are phosphorising: "These eggs of fire finally merged together with a very soft amorphous white paste, characterized by their extreme elasticity. Technical objects were to become my biggest enemy later on, and as for watches, they had to be soft or not at all."[2]
Dalí's life is overshadowed by the death of his brother. On August 1st, 1903, the first-born child of the family, scarcely two years old, died from gastroenteritis.

1. ***Port of Cadaqués*** *(Night)*, 1919.
Oil on canvas.
18.7 x 24.2 cm.
The Salvador Dali Museum,
St Petersburg (FL).

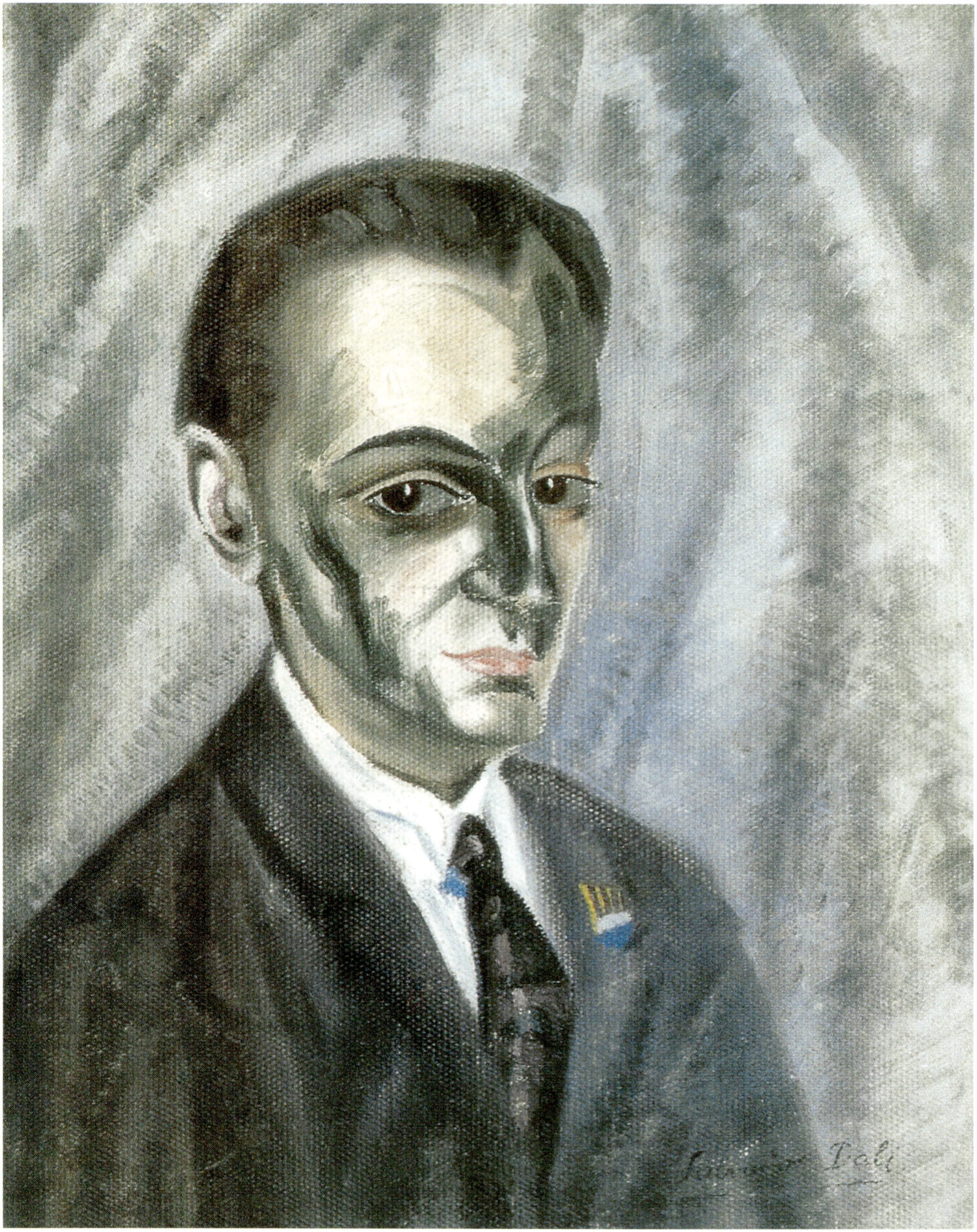

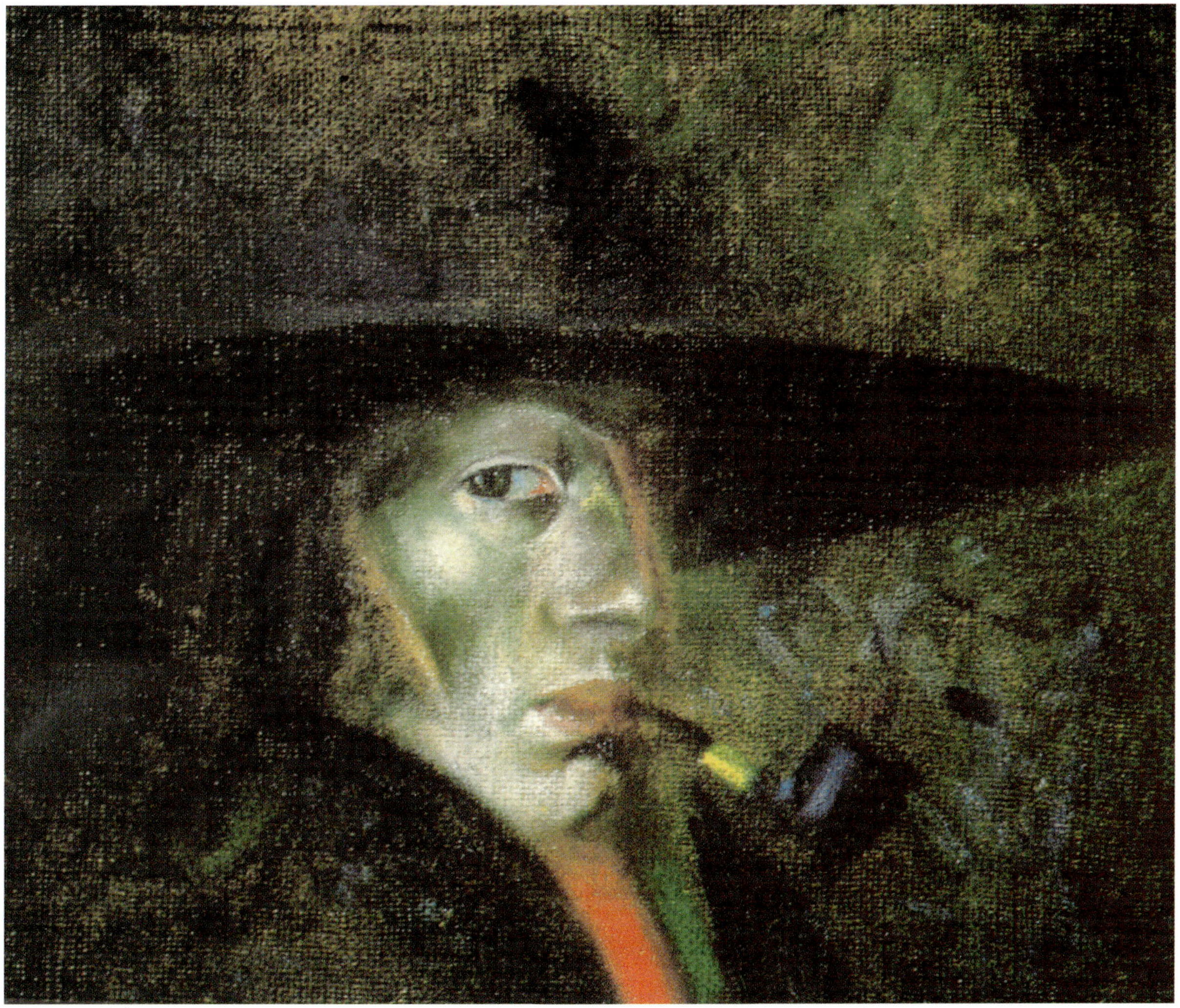

2. ***Portrait of José Torres***, c. 1920. Oil on canvas. 49.5 x 39.5 cm. Museum of Modern Art, Barcelona.

3. ***Self-Portrait***, c. 1921. Oil on canvas. 36.8 x 41.8 cm. The Salvador Dali Museum, St Petersburg (FL).

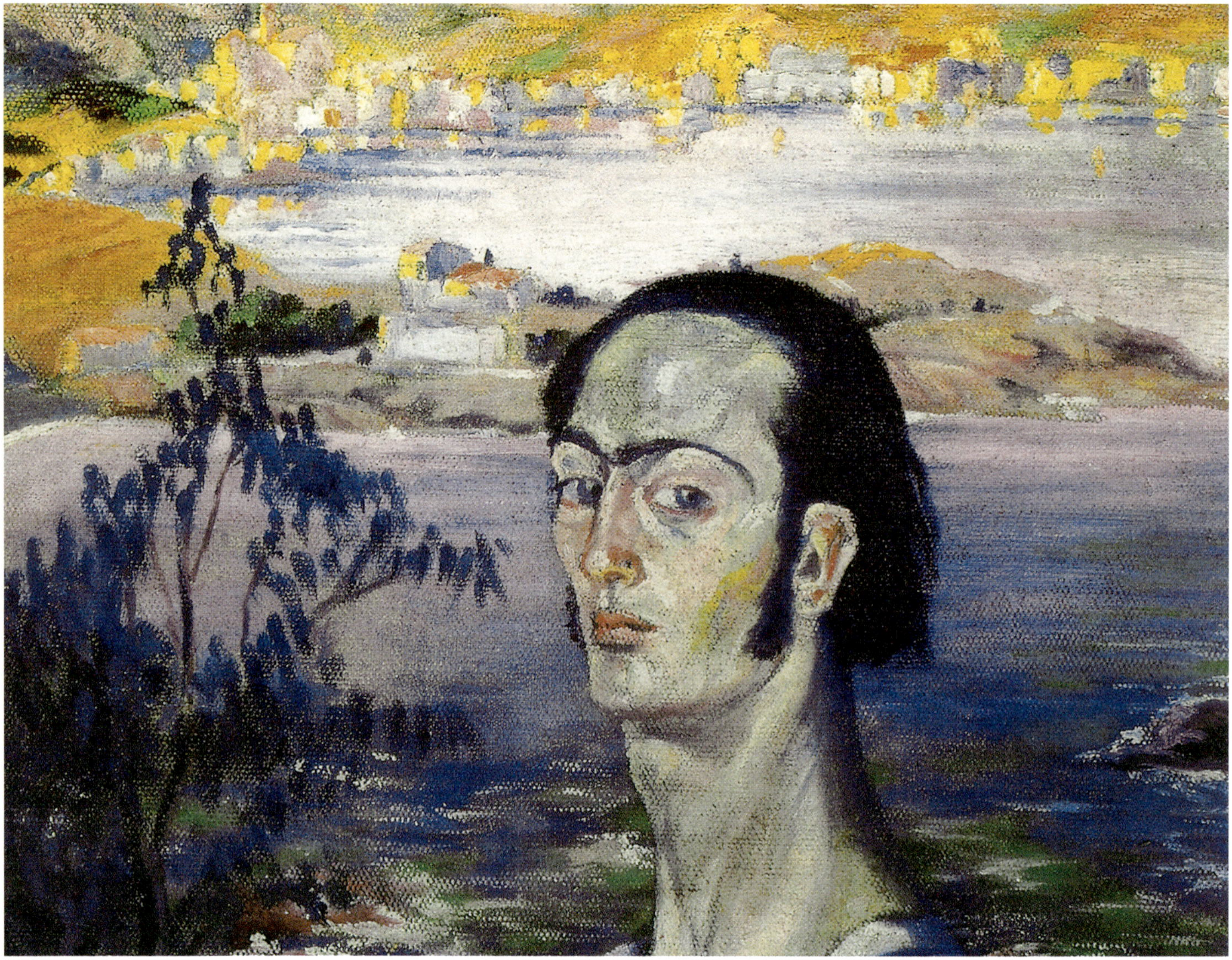

4. ***Self-Portrait with the Neck of Raphaël***, 1920-1921. Oil on canvas. 41.5 x 53 cm. The Gala-Salavdor Dali Foundation, Figueras.

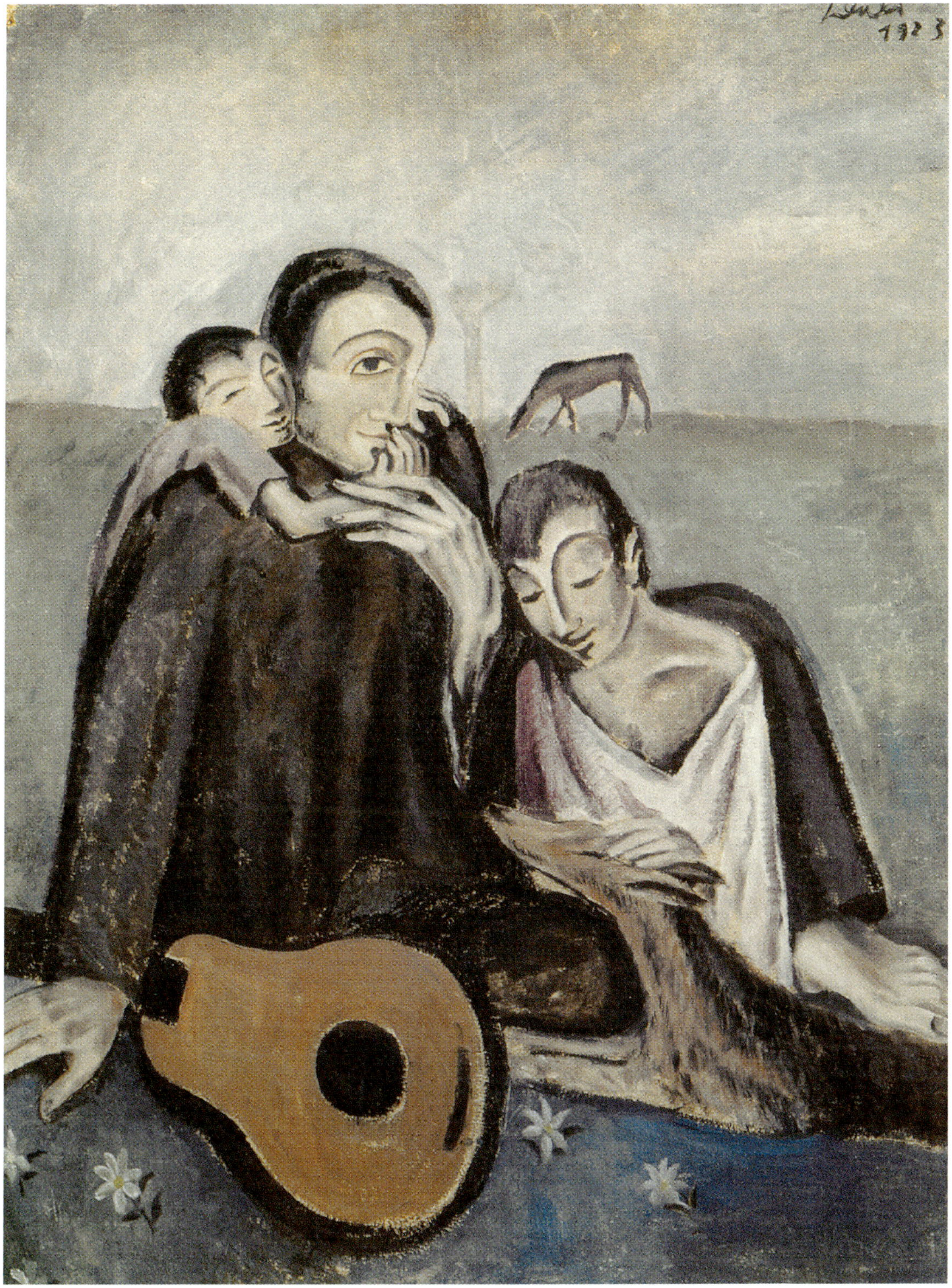

5. ***Family Scene***, 1923.
Oil and gouache on cardboard.
105 x 75 cm.
The Gala-Salvador Dali Foundation, Figueras.

The child Salvador sees himself as nothing more than a substitute for the dead brother: "Throughout the whole of my childhood and youth I lived with the perception that I was a part of my dead brother. That is, in my body and my soul, I carried the clinging carcass of this dead brother because my parents were constantly speaking about the other Salvador."[3]

Out of fear that the second-born child could also sicken and die, Salvador was particularly cosseted and spoiled. He was surrounded by a cocoon of female attention, not just spun by his mother Felipa Doménech Ferrés, but also later by his grandmother Maria Ana Ferrés and his aunt Catalina. Dalí reported that his mother continually admonished him to wear a scarf when he went outdoors. If he got sick, he enjoyed being allowed to remain in bed. Dalí's sister Ana Maria, four years younger, writes in her book, *Salvador Dalí visto por su hermana* (*Salvador Dalí, Seen Through the Eyes of his Sister*), that their mother only rarely let Salvador out of her sight and frequently kept watch at his bedside at night, for when he suddenly awoke, startled out of sleep, to find himself alone, he would start a terrible fuss.

Salvador enjoyed the company of the women and especially that of the eldest, his grandmother and Lucia. He had very little contact with children of his own age. He often played alone. He would disguise himself as a king and observe himself in the mirror: "With my crown, a cape thrown over my shoulders, and otherwise completely naked. Then I pressed my genitals back between my thighs, in order to look as much like a girl as possible. Even then I admired three things: weakness, age and luxury."[4]

Dalí's mother loved him unreservedly, even lionized him. With his father, Dalí enjoyed a different type of relationship. Salvador Dalí y Cusi was a notary in the Catalan market-town of Figueras, near the Spanish-French border. An anti-Catholic free thinker, he decided not to send his son Salvador to a church school, as would have befitted his social status, but to a state school. Only when Salvador failed to reach the required standard in the first year did his father allow him to transfer to a Catholic private school of the French "La Salle" order. There, among other things, the eight-year-old learned French, which was later to become his second mother tongue, and received his first lessons in painting and drawing. At about the same time as Salvador was receiving his first lessons from the brothers of the "La Salle" Order, he set-up his first atelier in the old, disused washroom in the attic of his family home: "I placed my chair in the concrete basin and arranged the high-standing wooden board (that protects washerwomen's clothing from the water) horizontally across it so that the basin was half covered. This was my workbench!"[5] Dalí's oldest existing works date from the year 1914. They are small-format watercolours, landscape studies of the area around Figueras.

6. ***Cubist Self-Portrait***, 1923. Gouache and collage on cardboard. 104.9 x 74.2 cm. Reina Sofia Art Centre, Madrid.

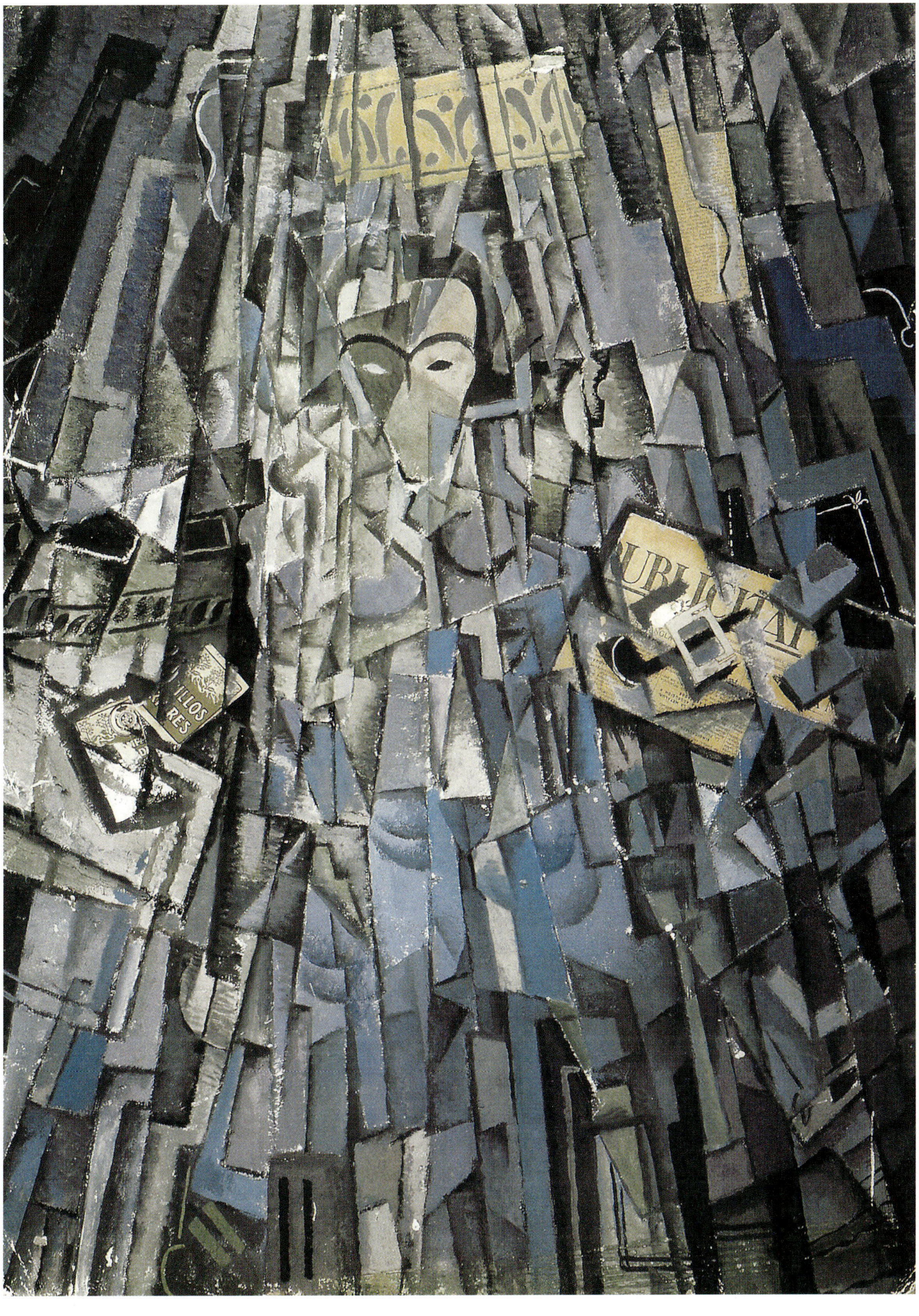

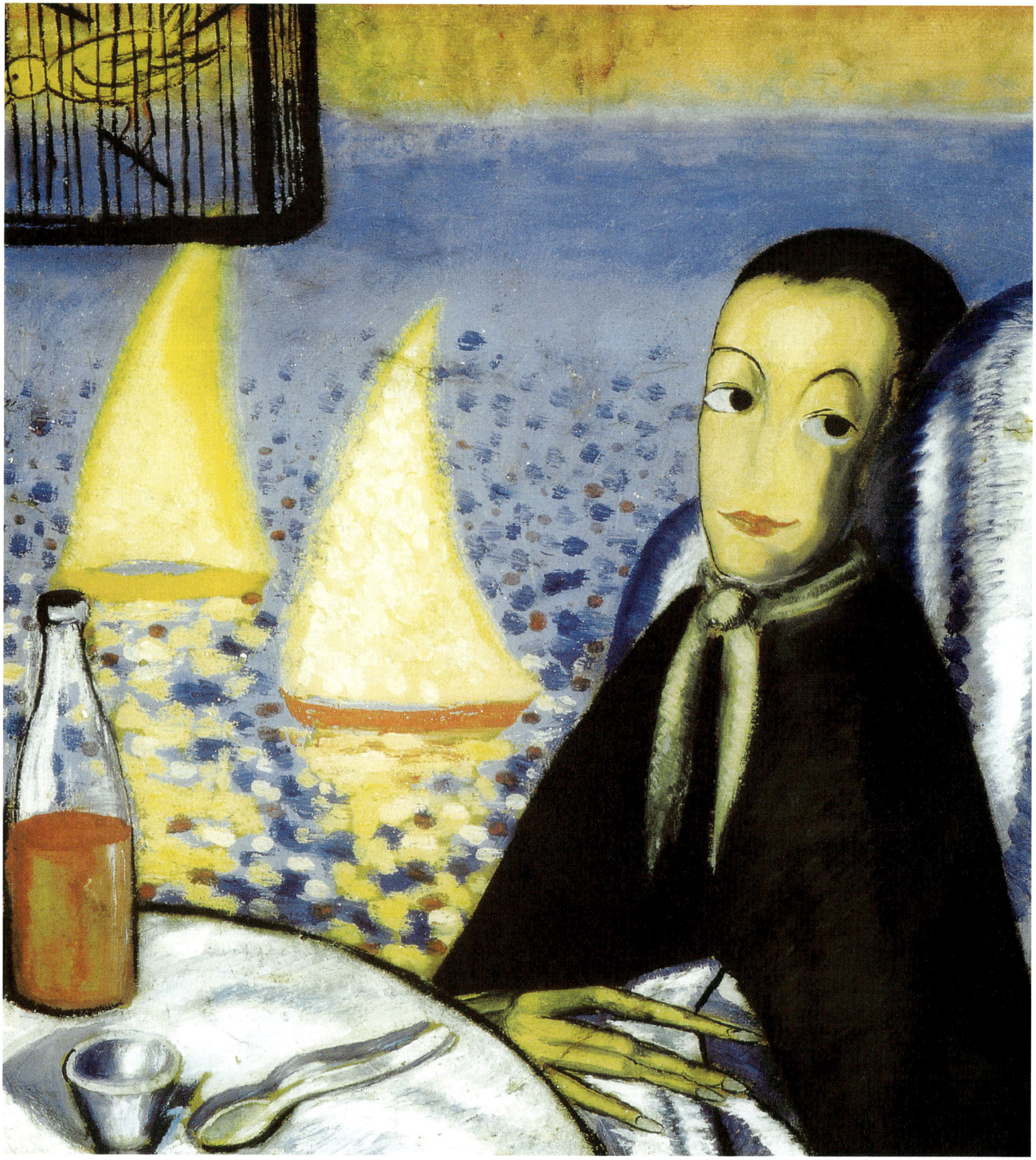

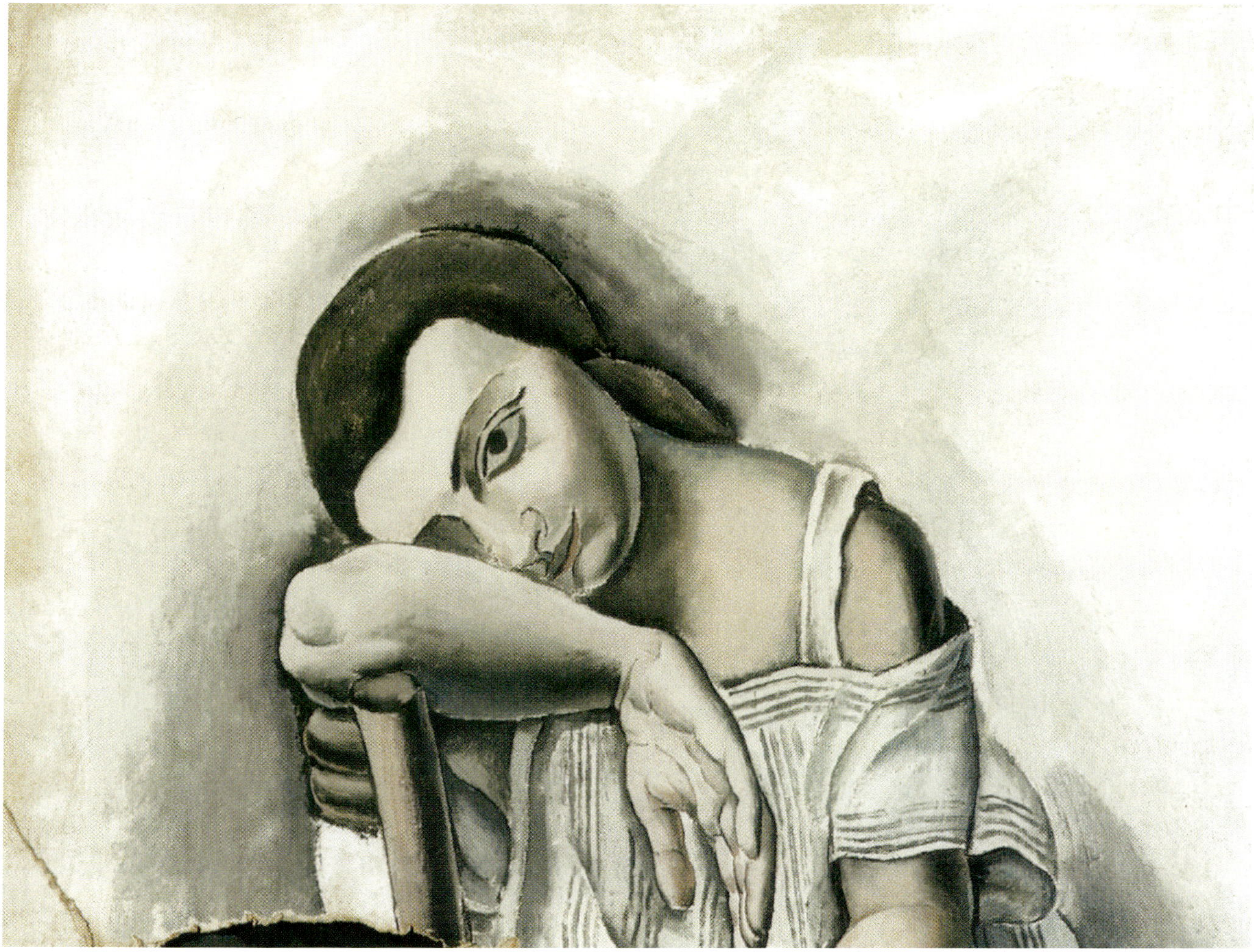

7. ***The Sick Child***, c. 1923. Oil and gouache on cardboard. 57 x 51 cm. The Salvador Dali Museum, St Petersburg (FL).

8. ***Portrait of Ana Maria***, c. 1924. Oil on cardboard. 55 x 75 cm. The Gala-Salvador Dali Foundation, Figueras.

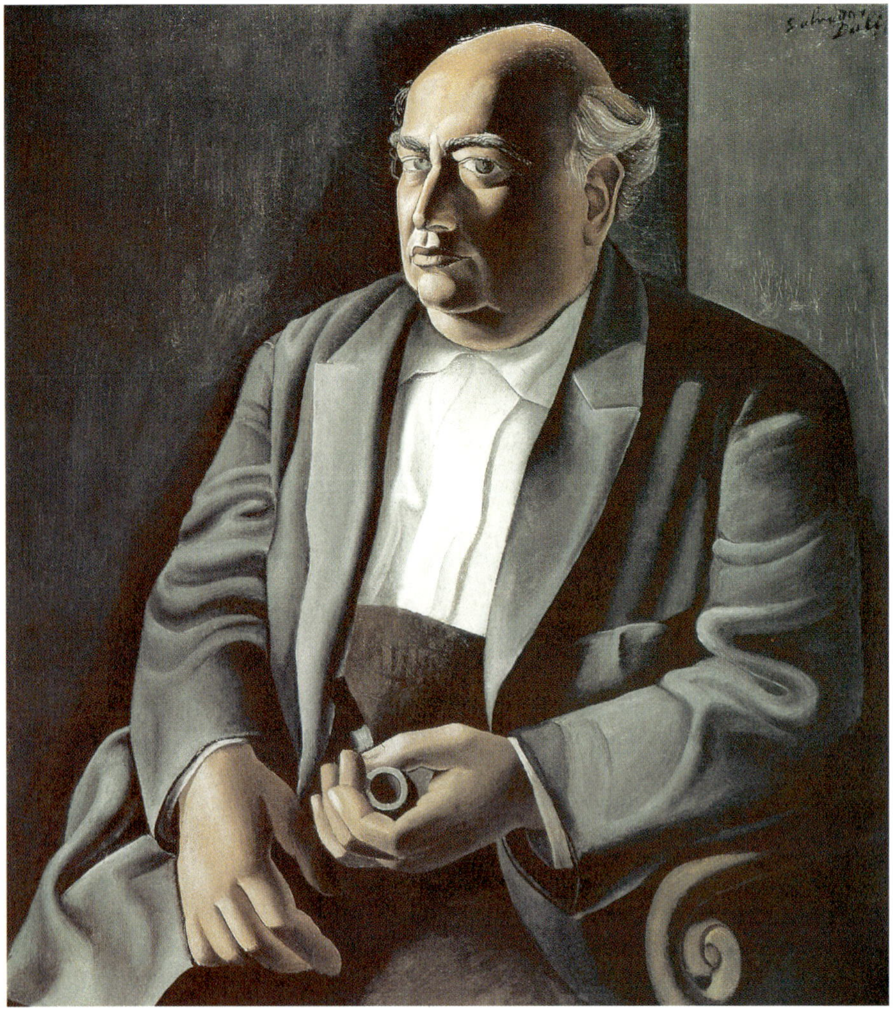

9. ***Portrait of my Father***, 1925.
Oil on canvas.
100 x 100 cm.
Museum of Modern Art, Barcelona.

10. ***Seated Girl from the Back***, 1925.
Oil on canvas.
103 x 73.5 cm.
Reina Sofia National Museum, Madrid.

Oil paintings by the eleven-year-old also exist, mostly as copies of masterpieces which he found in his father's well-stocked collection of art books. For Salvador, the atelier became the "sanctuary" of his loneliness. In the laundry-room atelier the little king tried out a new costume: "I started to test myself and to observe; as I performed hilarious eye-winking antics accompanied by a subliminal spiteful smile, at the edge of my mind, I knew, vague as it was, that I was in the process of playing the role of a genius. Ah Salvador Dalí! You know it now: if you play the role of a genius, you will also become one!" Later Dalí analysed his behavior: "In order to wrest myself from my dead brother, I had to play the genius so as to ensure that at every moment I was not in fact him, that I was not dead; as such, I was forced to put on all sorts of eccentric poses."[6]

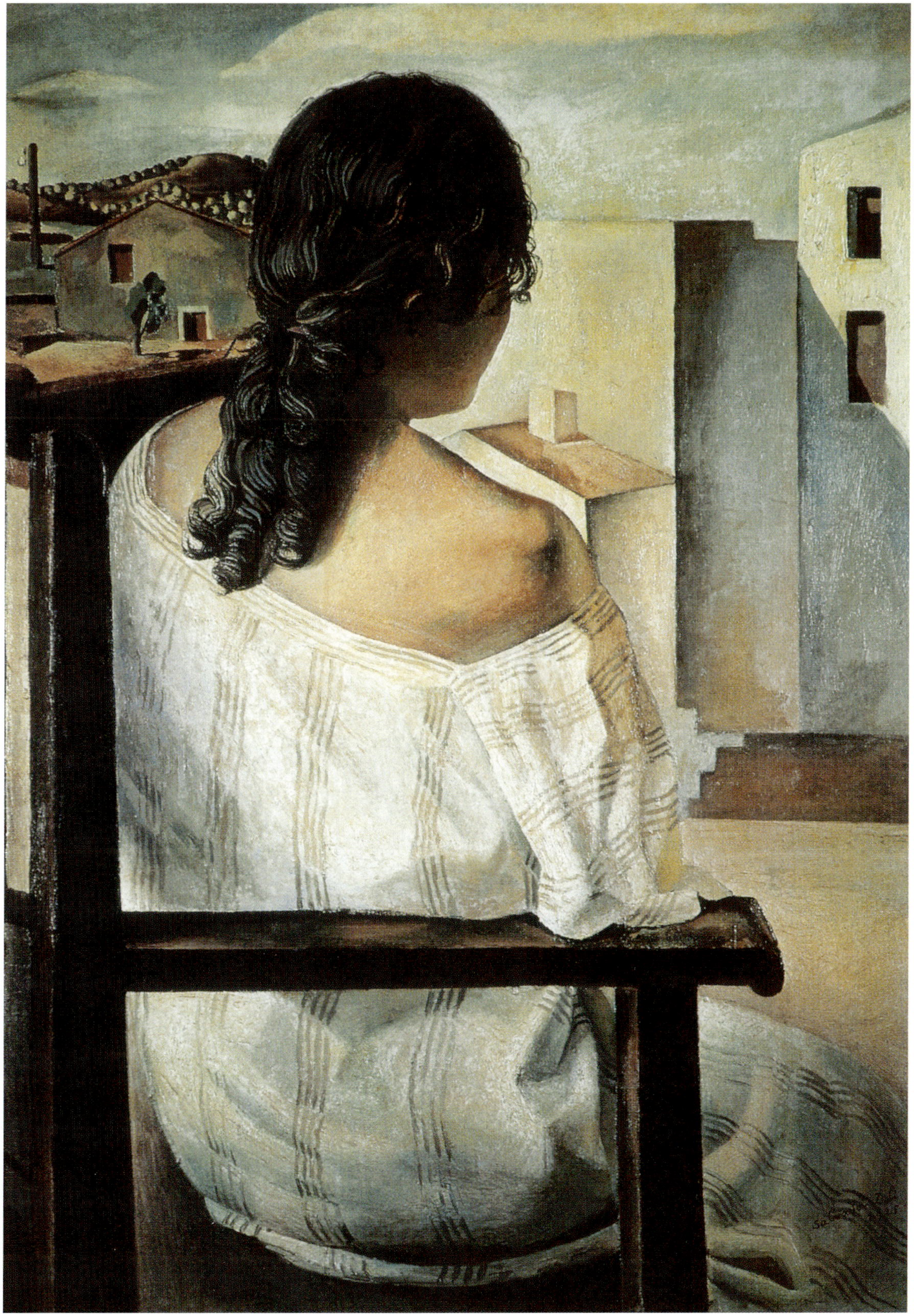

Salvador's attempts to distance himself from his dead brother went so far that he believed himself immortal. Descending the stairs one day at school, it suddenly occured to him that he should let himself fall. But at the very last moment fear held him back. However, he worked out a plan of action for the next day: "At the very moment I was descending the stairs with all my classmates, I did a fantastic leap into the void, and landing on the steps below bowled over and over until I finally reached the bottom. The effect on the other boys and the teachers who ran over to help me was enormous."[7]
The ability to attract the attention of the others, and to be subsequently admired by them afforded the little king Salvador untold enjoyment. However, he did prefer it when his "entourage" kept their distance. From his window in the laundry-room atelier he spied on the other children, particularly the schoolgirls from the neighbouring school.
In the summer of 1916, the twelve-year-old was sent on holiday to the estate of some family friends, the Pitchots. The "Mulí de la Torre" estate, named after its tower-mill, and just a few kilometers from Figueras, was to become a place of magic for Salvador. For weeks he gave himself up to his day-dreams undisturbed, a reverie for which he only had the odd single hour in Figueras in his laundry-room atelier. Most of his fantasies at this time were of an erotic nature. Eroticism and death become unified very early in Dalí's life.
From a net of fantasies centered around eroticism, death, and disgust, Dalí only managed to save himself by his own mental agility. During puberty, and wholly without any system, he began to read through his father's extensive library. He occupied himself especially with the philosophers Voltaire, Nietzsche, Descartes, and Spinoza; but without doubt his favourite was Kant: "I loved very much to lose myself in the labyrinth of his avenues of thought, in which the ever expanding crystals of my youthful intelligence found true heavenly music reflected."[8]
Despite this monopolisation by philosophy, Dalí also occupied himself with art history and continued his attempts at painting. His father supported him by buying him canvas, brushes, paints and magazines. However, a more important role as sponsor was taken over by Pepito Pitchot, who set up for him an atelier in a barn. Dalí painted landscapes in the impressionist style and he also developed his own ideas. One day, for example, he attached real cherry-stems to his paintings of cherries. Pepito Pitchot was impressed by this idea; so much so that he promised to talk Señor Dalí into allowing Salvador to receive lessons in painting. In the coming school year Dalí changed to the private Marist high school. In addition, he visited Juan Nuñez's painting class at the city art school. As Dalí later stated, he owed much to this teacher. By this time the boy was convinced that he wanted to become a painter.

11. ***Figure at a Window***, 1925. Oil on canvas. 103 x 75 cm. Reina Sofia National Museum, Madrid.

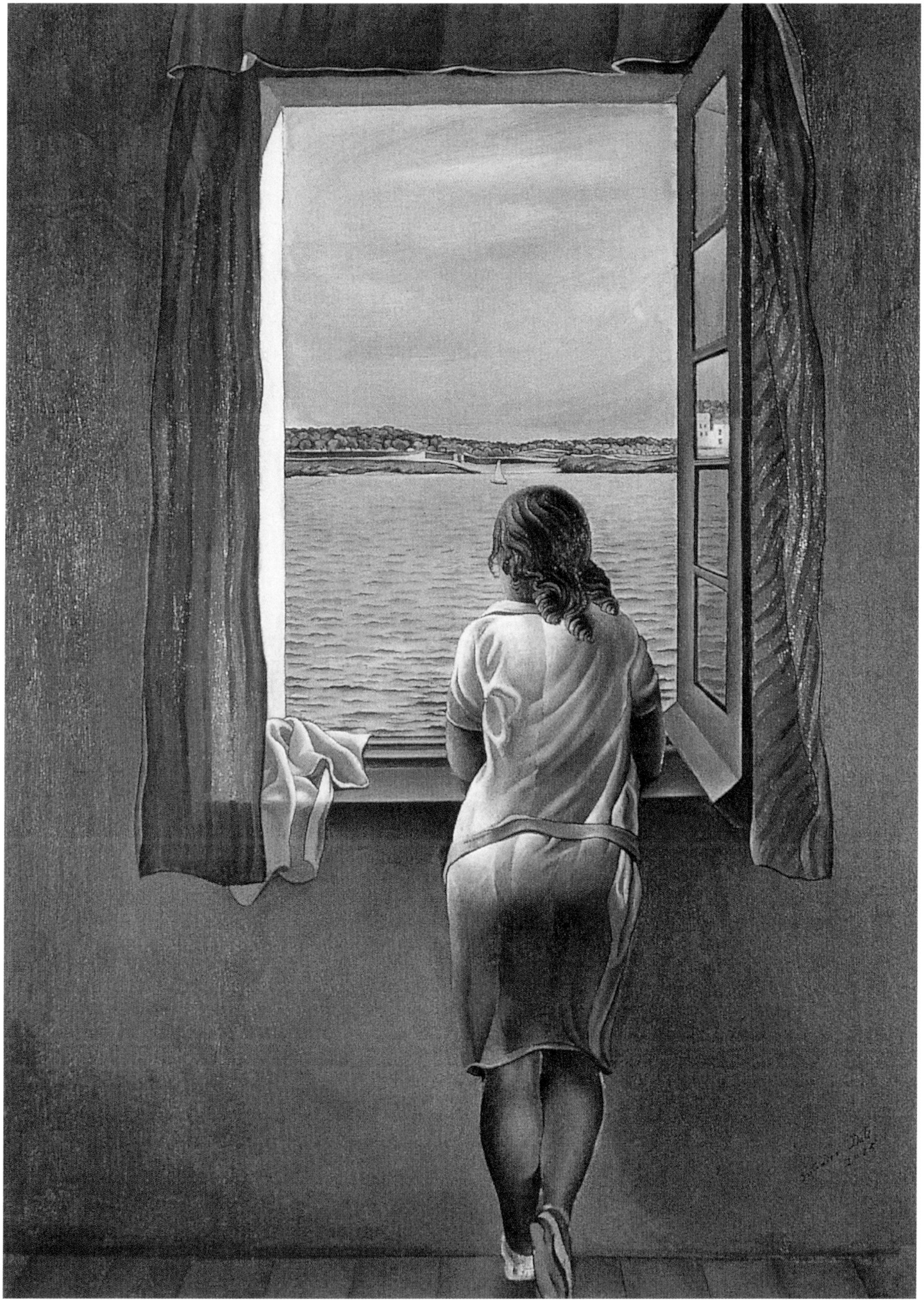

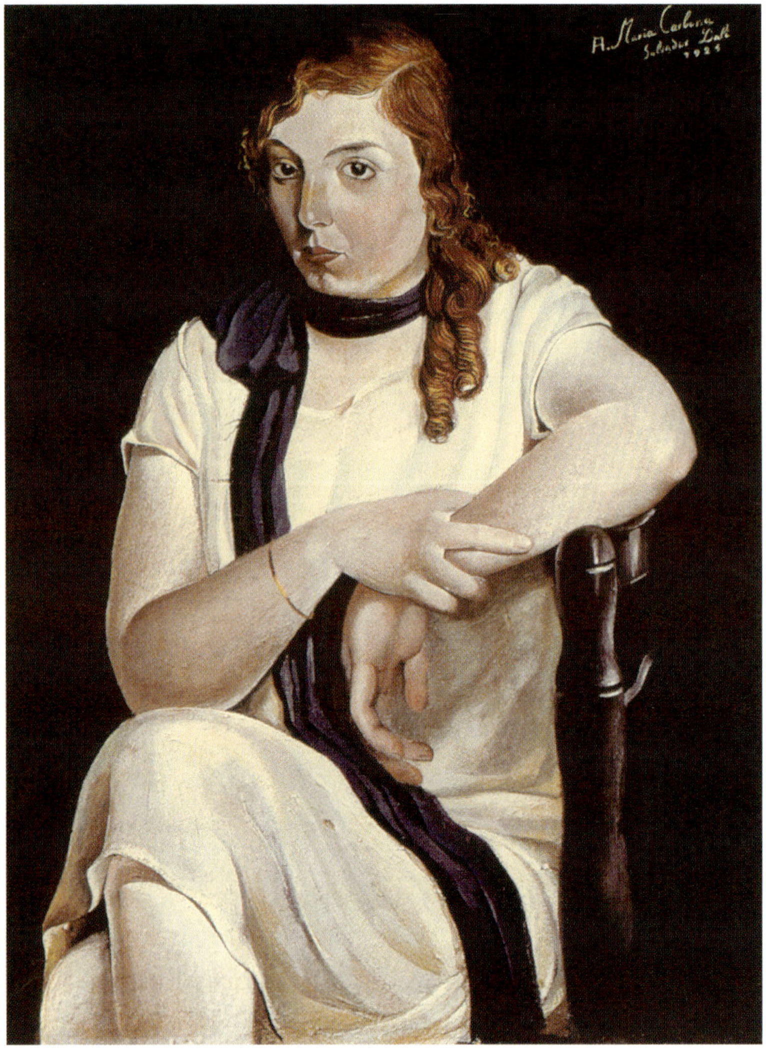

12. ***Portrait of Maria Carbona***, 1925.
Oil on panel.
52.6 x 39.2 cm.
Museum of Fine Arts,
Montréal.

13. ***Girl from the Back***,
1926. Oil on panel.
32 x 27 cm.
The Salvador Dali Museum,
St Petersburg (FL).

Fundamentally, his father had nothing against this; however he insisted on a formal training: first the high school diploma, then study at the vocational school of art, sculpture and graphics in Madrid. Dalí spent the summer of 1919 in Cadaqués, his father's birthplace on the Costa Brava.
The family had a little holiday house there. Cadaqués was a place which Dalí loved "with fanatical loyalty" the whole of his life.
On February 6th, 1921, Felipa Doménech died. Dalí's father promptly married his deceased wife's sister, Catalin, who had already been living in his household for the last eleven years.

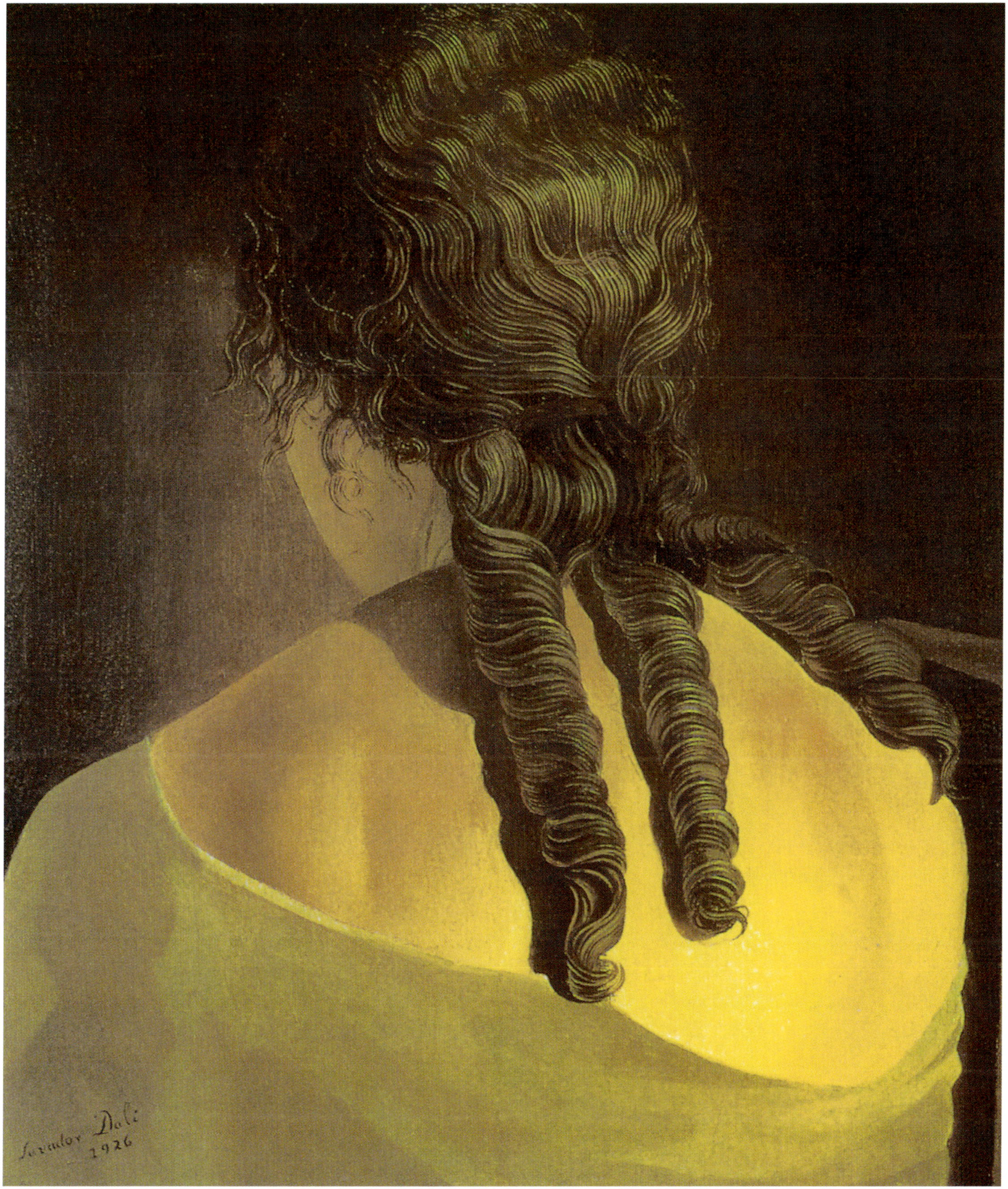
Salvador Dalí
1926

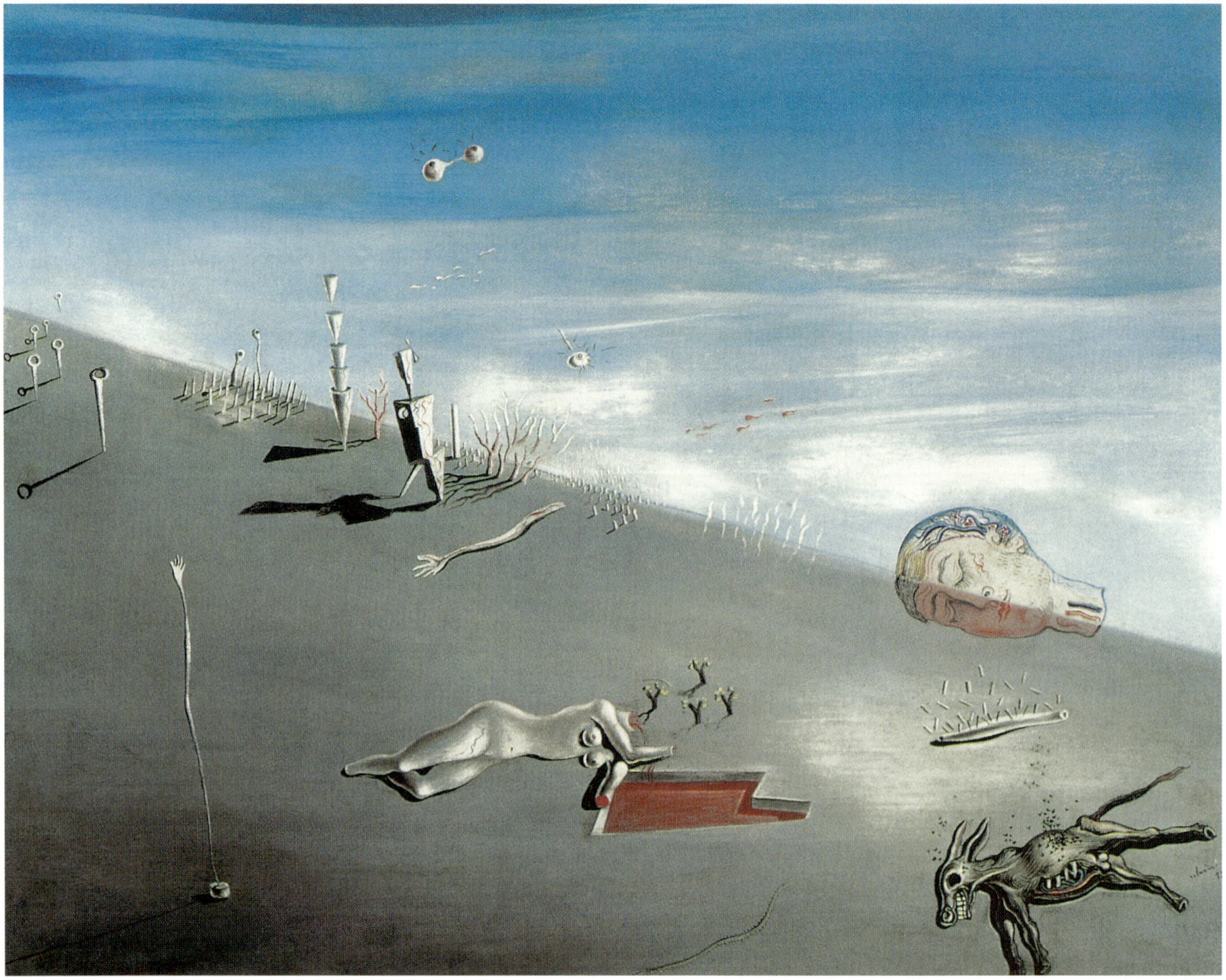

14. ***Study for Honey is Sweeter than Blood***, 1926. Oil on panel. 25.1 x 32.6 cm. Museum of Modern Art, New York.

15. ***The Girl of Ampurdan***, 1926. Oil on plywood. 51 x 40 cm. The Salvador Dali Museum, St Petersburg (FL).

For Dalí, the death of his mother was "the worst blow of my whole life. I worshipped her; for me she was unique. [...] Weeping and with clenched teeth I swore that with all the power of the holy light which one day would circle my glorious name I would rescue my mother from death and from fate."[9]

The sixteen-year-old planned his fame in detail: first he wanted to go to the vocational school of art, sculpture, and graphics in Madrid for three years, win a prize, and then continue his studies in Italy. Before departing for Madrid after having successfully completed his high school diploma, Dalí presented eight paintings at a group exhibition held by the Catalan student union in Barcelona's Dalmau gallery.

In the local press the young painter was confirmed as having extraordinary talent: "Dalí is on the road to great success."[10]

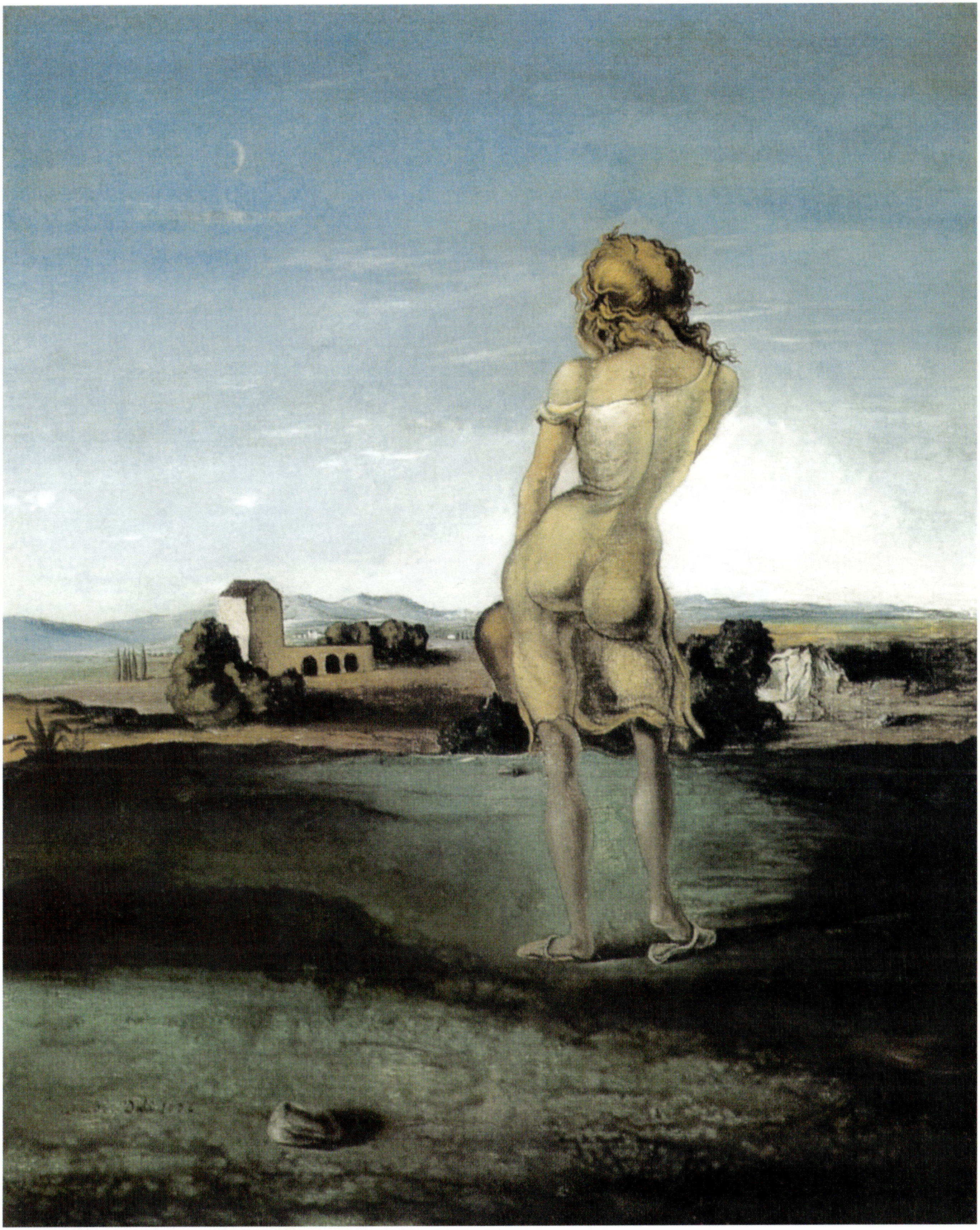

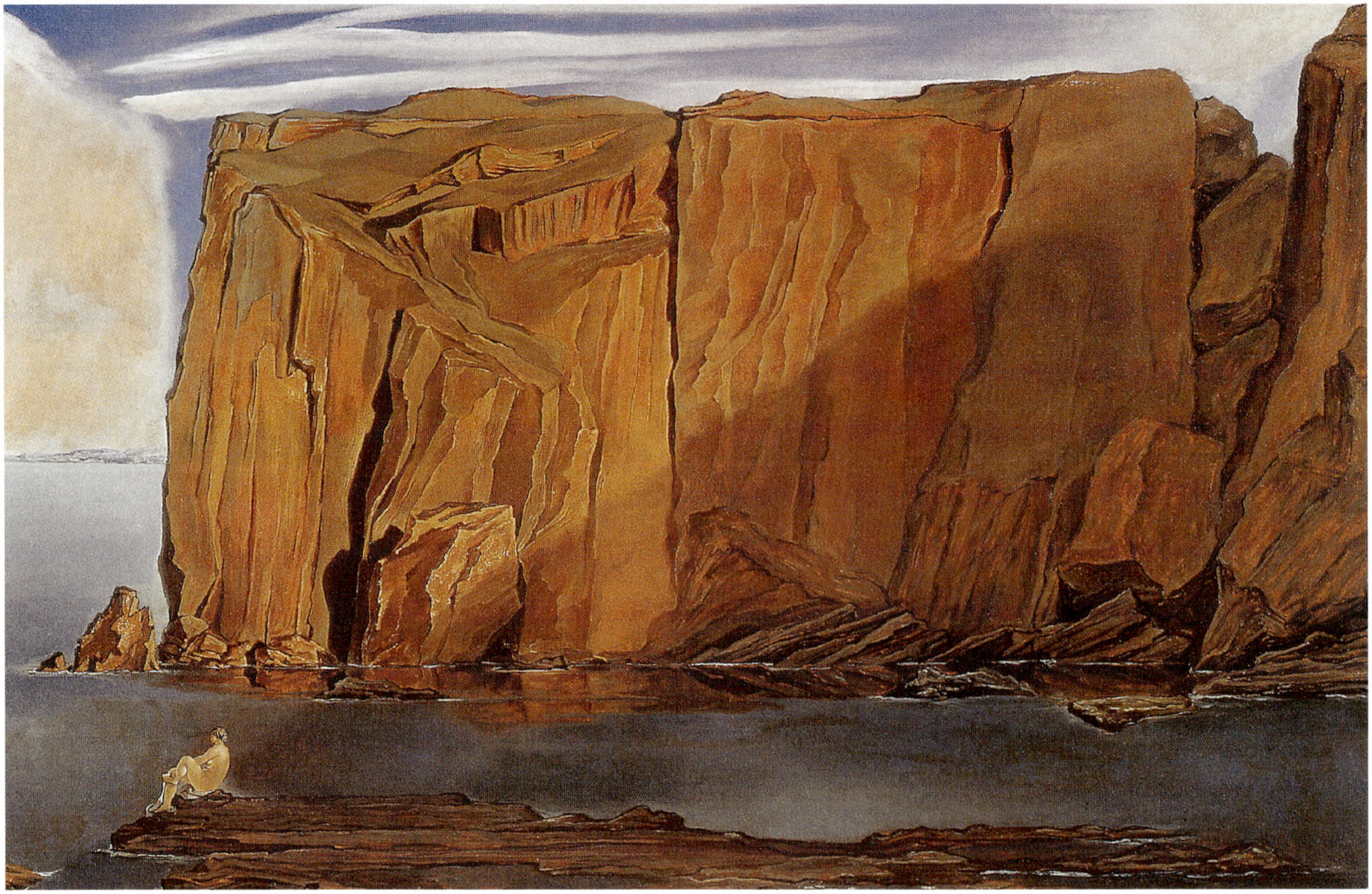

16. ***Penya-Segats** (Woman on the Rocks)*, 1926.
Oil on olive panel.
26 x 40 cm.
Private collection.

From Outsider to Dandy. The Student Years in Madrid

In the autumn of 1922, accompanied by his father and his sister Ana Maria, the eighteen-year-old traveled to the entrance examination at the art school in Madrid. For over six days, the applicants had to prepare a drawing of a classical sculpture. Dalí's model was a cast of Bacchus after Jacopo Sansovino. Dalí moved into a room at the "Residencia de Estudiantes", a student residential and cultural centre based on the Oxford and Cambridge model. At the beginning of the twenties a group of Spain's literary and artistic offspring lived there; amongst others, Luis Buñuel, Federico Garcia Lorca, Pedro Garfias, Eugenio Montes, and Pepin Bello. Dalí kept to himself and cultivated his role as a loner: he let his hair grow long, and dressed himself in short trousers, a long cape and a big, black felt hat. In the morning he attended his courses at the academy, and in the afternoon and evening he worked in his room.

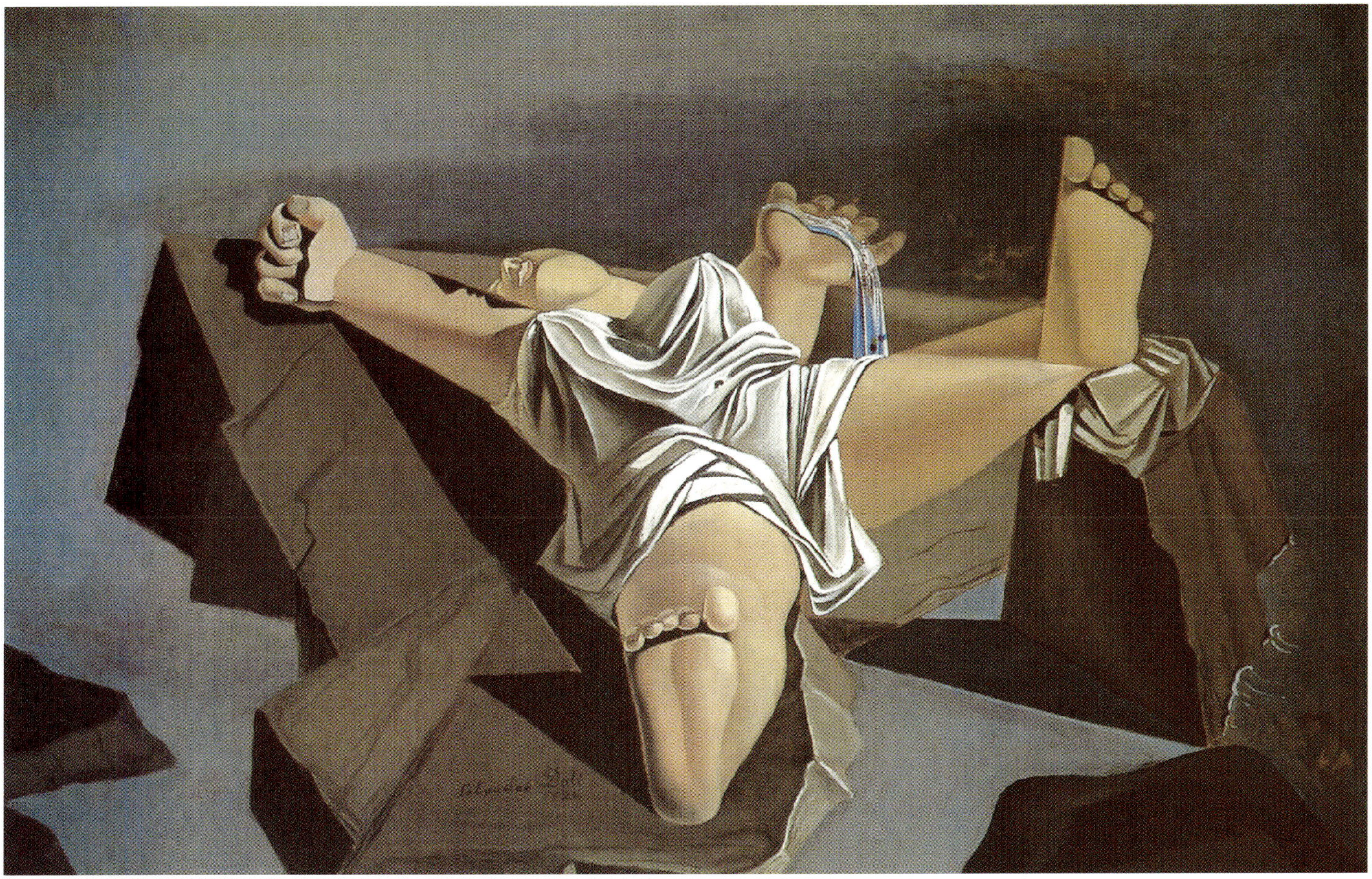

The young student did not hold many of his teachers at the academy in very high esteem; for him they were too modern. " I had expected barriers, sternness, and science. Instead I was offered freedom, laziness, new approaches!"[11] At the same time Dalí criticized the professors for their inability to let go of French Impressionism, and their lack of attention to the newer developments in art, such as Cubism. In his private studies, Dalí read the writings of Georges Braque and bought reproductions of his pictures. He attempted to apply the new teachings on form to canvas. One day, one of his fellow students, Pepin Bello, discovered two Cubistic paintings in his room. Bello belonged to a literary-artistic circle, and he informed them of his findings immediately. Up to this point Dalí had been considered a reactionary eccentric. Of all people, nobody had suspected that he could be so well-informed of the newest events in Paris, the great art metropolis. Dalí's life changed following this discovery. The interest the others showed in him suddenly transformed him: the lone wolf metamorphosed and a dandy was born.

17. ***Figure on the Rocks*** *(Sleeping Woman)*, 1926. Oil on plywood. 27 x 41 cm. The Salvador Dali Museum, St Petersburg (FL).

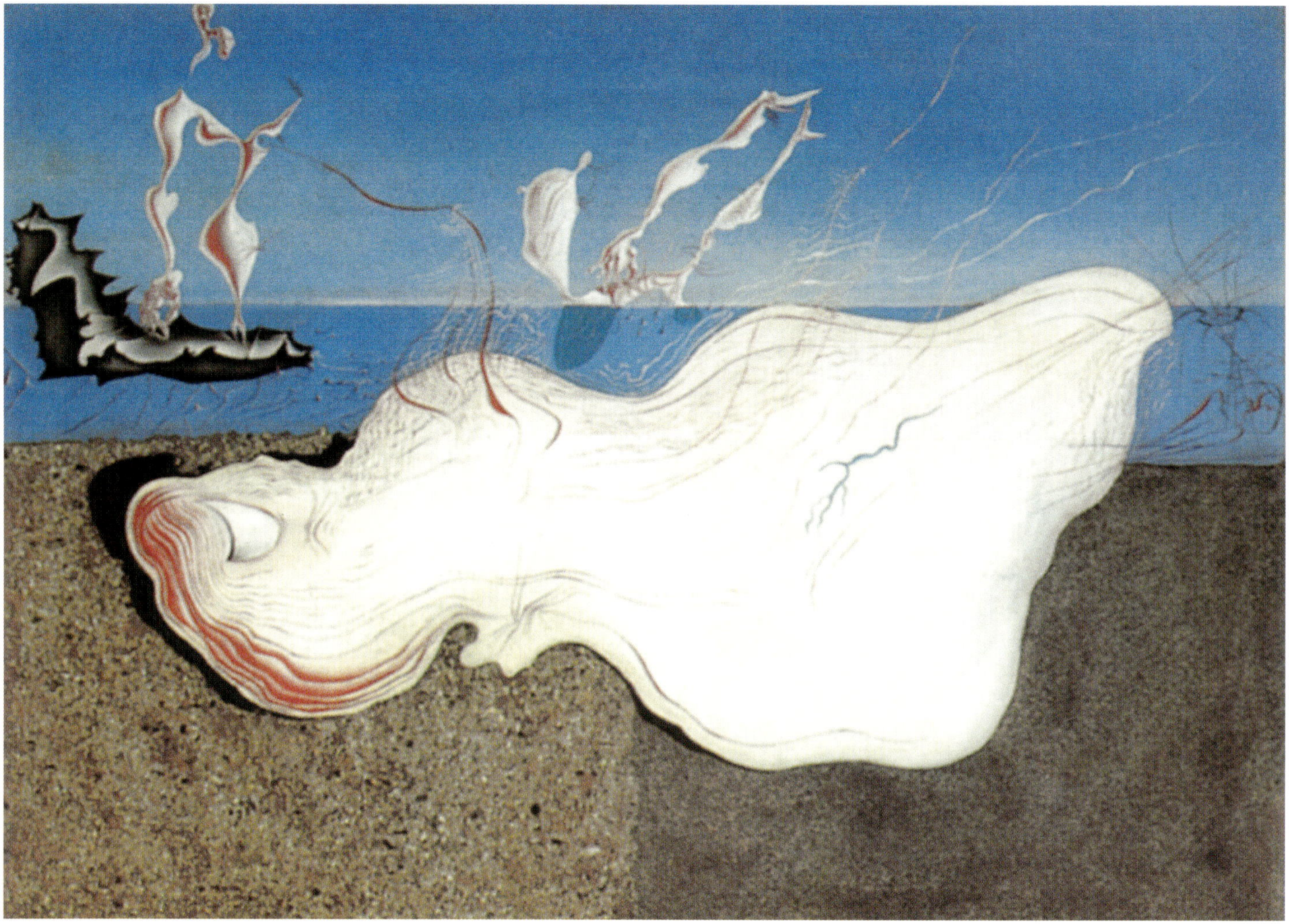

18. ***Bather***, 1928.
Oil, sand and gravel collage on panel.
52 x 71.7 cm.
The Salvador Dali Museum,
St Petersburg (FL).

19. ***Little Cinders*** *(Cenicitas)*, 1927-1928. Oil on panel. 64 x 48 cm.
The Reina Sofia National Museum, Madrid.

He cut his hair and bought the most expensive suit he could find at the most elegant men's outfitter's in Madrid.
After four months of living like an ascetic, Dalí began to live the life of a Bohemian. Instead of attending painting-classes he now went to restaurants and bars. In the literary-artistic circles at the Café de Pombo he met Luis Buñuel who was, later to become a film director, and the poet Federico Garcia Lorca. At the beginning of his second year of studies, Dalí was gated from the academy for twelve months. Exclusion from classes did not trouble him. He firmly believed that the professors were incapable of teaching him anything. He remained in Madrid and began to study sketching nudes at the "Free Academy", which had been founded previously by the painter Julio Moisés.

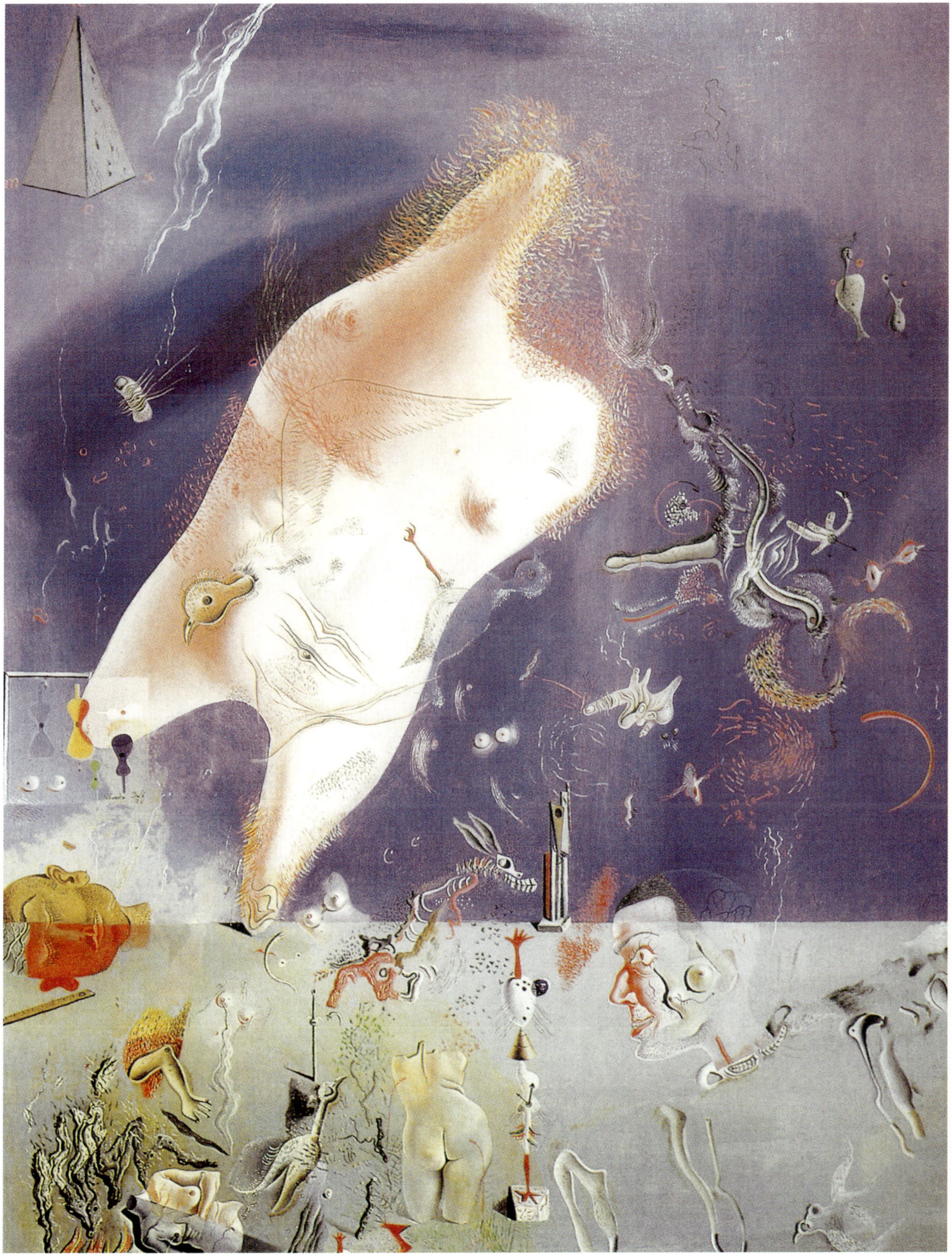

At the beginning of 1924 he returned to Figueras. His sister, Ana Maria, became his preferred model. He painted rear views of her either standing or sitting at the open window. In May 1925, he took part in the First Iberian Artists' Art-Salon with ten paintings, amongst them a portrait of his friend Luis Buñuel that he had painted in 1924. In November, the Dalmau gallery in Barcelona presented the first one man show of Dalí's paintings.
Among the most renowned visitors at the exhibition was Pablo Picasso. The forty-one-year-old was especially taken by the painting *Young Girl Standing at a Window*. Six months later, Dalí travelled to Paris and visited his famous countryman: "As I entered Picasso's apartment in the rue de la Boétie, I was so deeply moved and full of respect, it was as if I was at an audience with the Pope. [...]We went up one floor, where Picasso showed me numerous pictures of his own for two hours. [...] Before showing me each new canvas he threw me a look of such vivaciousness and intelligence that I began to tremble."[12] Dalí's high regard for Picasso did not last long. Later he was to claim that just one of his own paintings was a thousand times better than the whole of Picasso's work altogether. Shortly after his return from Paris, the final examinations took place at the art school. Dalí denounced the examination commission as not being qualified to assess him. He was, once more, banished from the academy and returned to Figueras.

A Friendship in Verse and Still-Life. Dalí and Garcia Lorca

Dalí and the poet Federico Garcia Lorca had met in 1923 in Madrid but their close friendship only developed in 1925 during the Easter holidays when they travelled to Figueras and Cadaqués together. At Dalí's home Garcia Lorca organised two readings from his first drama, *Mariana Pineda*. After his departure, a lively correspondence developed between Garcia Lorca and Dalí and also with Ana Maria. Garcia Lorca wrote to her using tender words. Later, Dalí claimed more than once that the poet's love had been directed at him alone: "He was a known homosexual and madly in love with me. He tried to have me twice."[13] But actually, Dalí's letters to Garcia Lorca take on another tone; they are still free of all the cynicism that will later become the trademark of the painter. From the correspondence between Dalí and Garcia Lorca, only the letters of the painter remain almost completely preserved, while most of the others were lost in the Civil War. In 1926, Garcia Lorca wrote *Ode to Salvador Dalí*: "But above all I sing of our mutual ideas that unite us in the dark and golden hours. Art is not the light that blinds our eyes. First it is love, or friendship or even the conflict."[14] The portrait *Still Life (Invitation to Sleep)* was painted in the same year.

20. ***Anthropomorphic Beach***, 1928.
Oil, cork, stone, red sponge and polychrome finger carved of wood on canvas.
47.5 x 27.5 cm.
The Salvador Dalí Museum,
St Petersburg (FL).

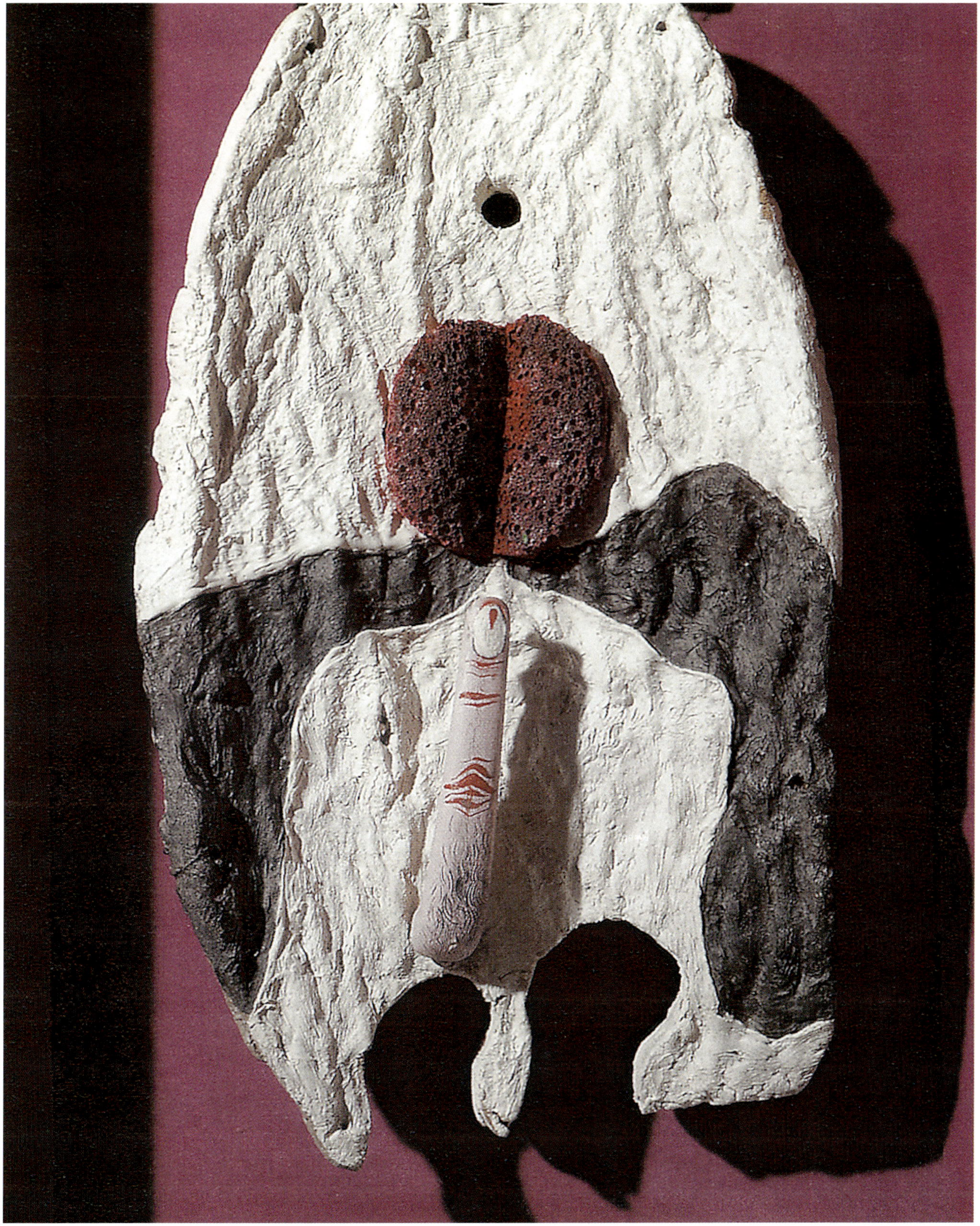

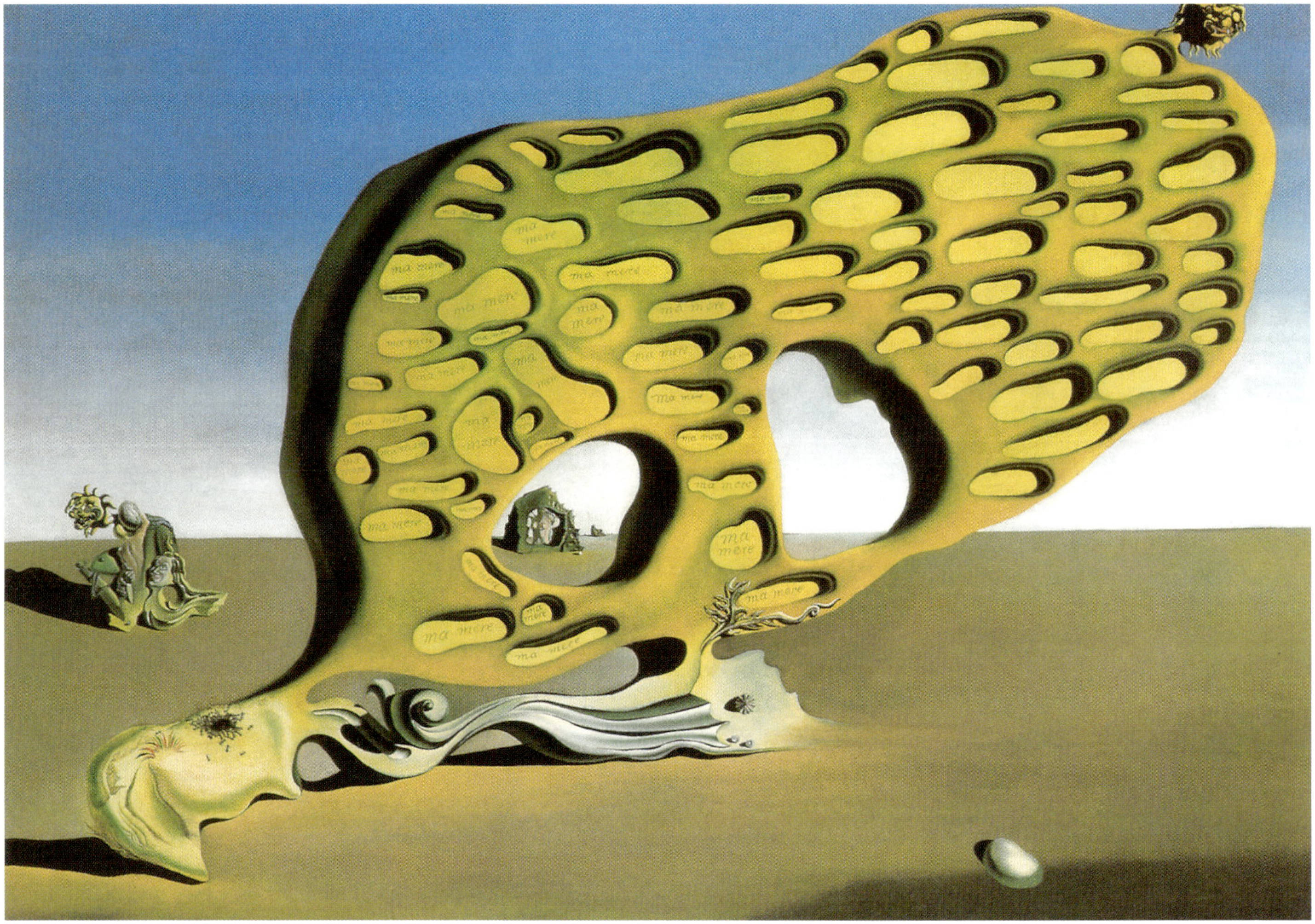

21. ***The Enigma of Desire – My Mother, my Mother, my Mother***, 1929.
Oil on canvas.
110 x 150.7 cm.
Gallery of Modern Art, Munich.

From a photo Ana Maria had taken of the sleeping poet in 1925, Dalí painted Garcia Lorca's head in the style of a Roman bust, where the plastic qualities in relief and outline are broken down into shadows and the portrayal of features. The poet and the painter do not only, in their respective work, make reference to one another - in 1926, they also began to work on a piece together: Dalí created the scenery and the costumes for the premiere of Garcia Lorca's *Mariana Pineda* in Barcelona. However, the date for the beginning of rehearsals at the Goya Theater was continually postponed. In the spring of 1927, Dalí impatiently wrote to Garcia Lorca "I await you every day."[15] In May of 1927, Garcia Lorca finally arrived in Figueras to finish the scenery with Dalí. The premiere took place on 24th June. Immediately afterwards, Garcia Lorca accompanied the Dalí family back to Cadaqués. This was the last summer that the friends spent together.

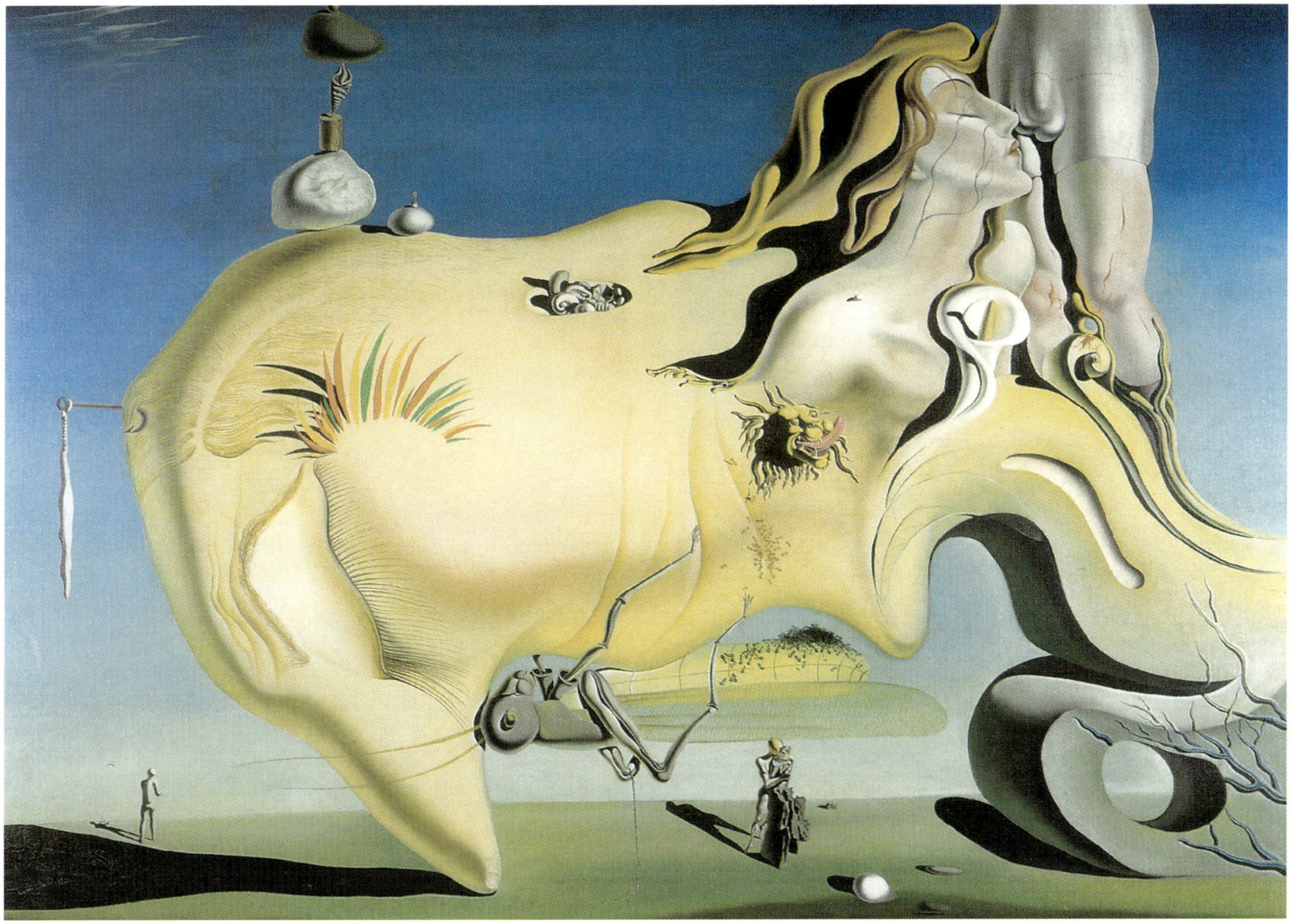

In the spring of 1928, Dalí drew the title-picture for *Gallo*, the magazine that Garcia Lorca published in Granada. However, the painter and the poet were both approaching a point in their lives where they would choose to take different directions. Dalí engaged himself in anti-art activities and joined the Surrealists; Garcia Lorca developed an ever-growing interest in folkart. In April of 1928, Garcia Lorca published his *Gypsy-Romance*. Shortly after the beginning of the Spanish Civil War, Garcia Lorca was murdered by Franco's soldiers. In 1966, Dalí described his reaction to the death of his young friend: "As I learnt of his death, I reacted like a bandit. Someone had brought me the newspaper, and realising that he had been executed by firing squad, I cried out: 'Olé'.[...] for Federico Garcia Lorca, I considered this to be the most beautiful death: to be mown down by the Civil War."[16]

22. ***The Great Masturbator***, 1929.
Oil on canvas.
110 x 150 cm.
The Reina Sofía National Museum, Madrid.

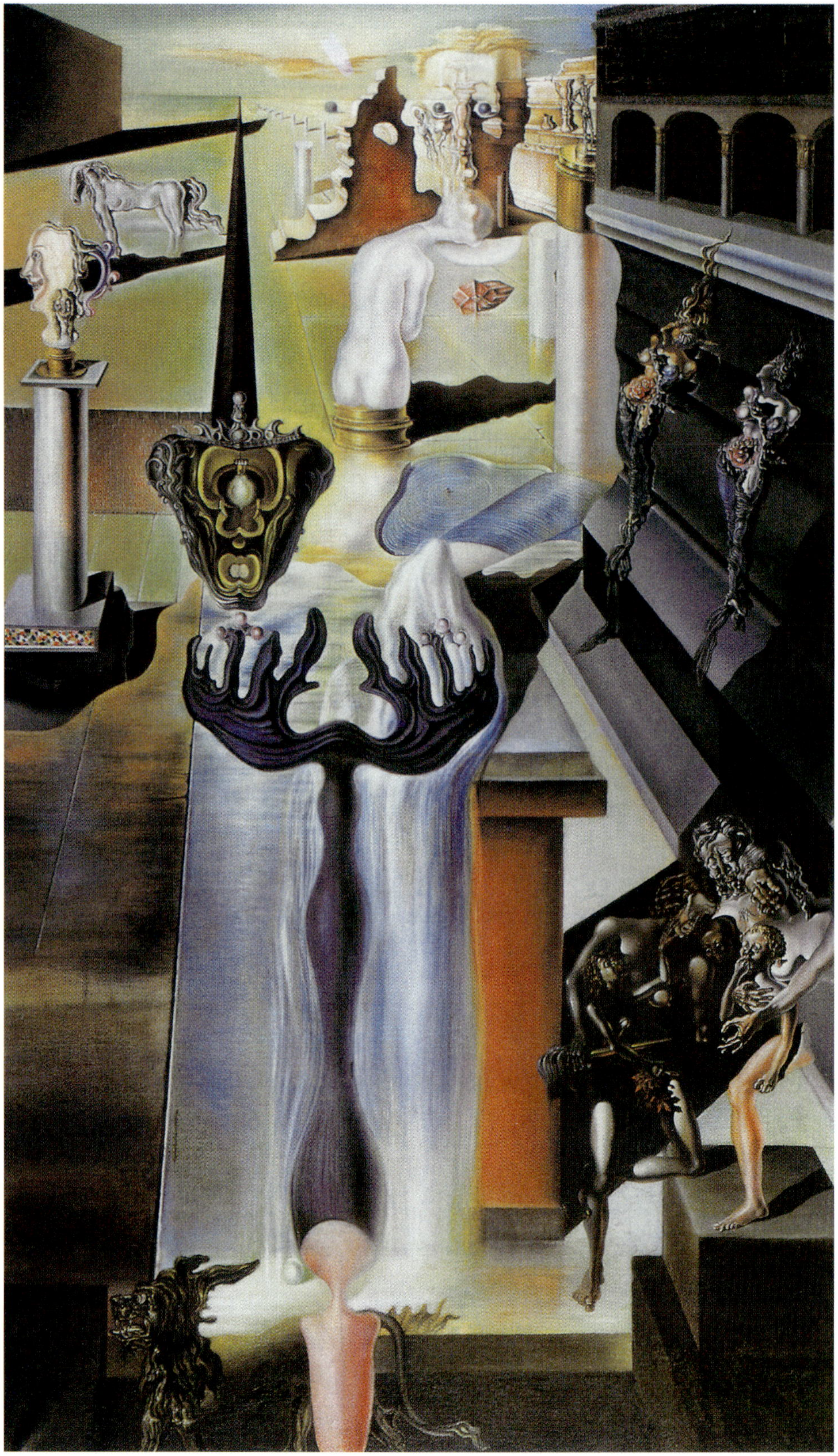

23. ***The Invisible Man***, 1929. Oil on canvas. 140 x 80 cm. The Reina Sofía National Museum, Madrid.

24. ***Portrait of Paul Éluard***, 1929. Oil on cardboard. 33 x 25 cm. Formerly The Gala-Salvador Dalí Collection.

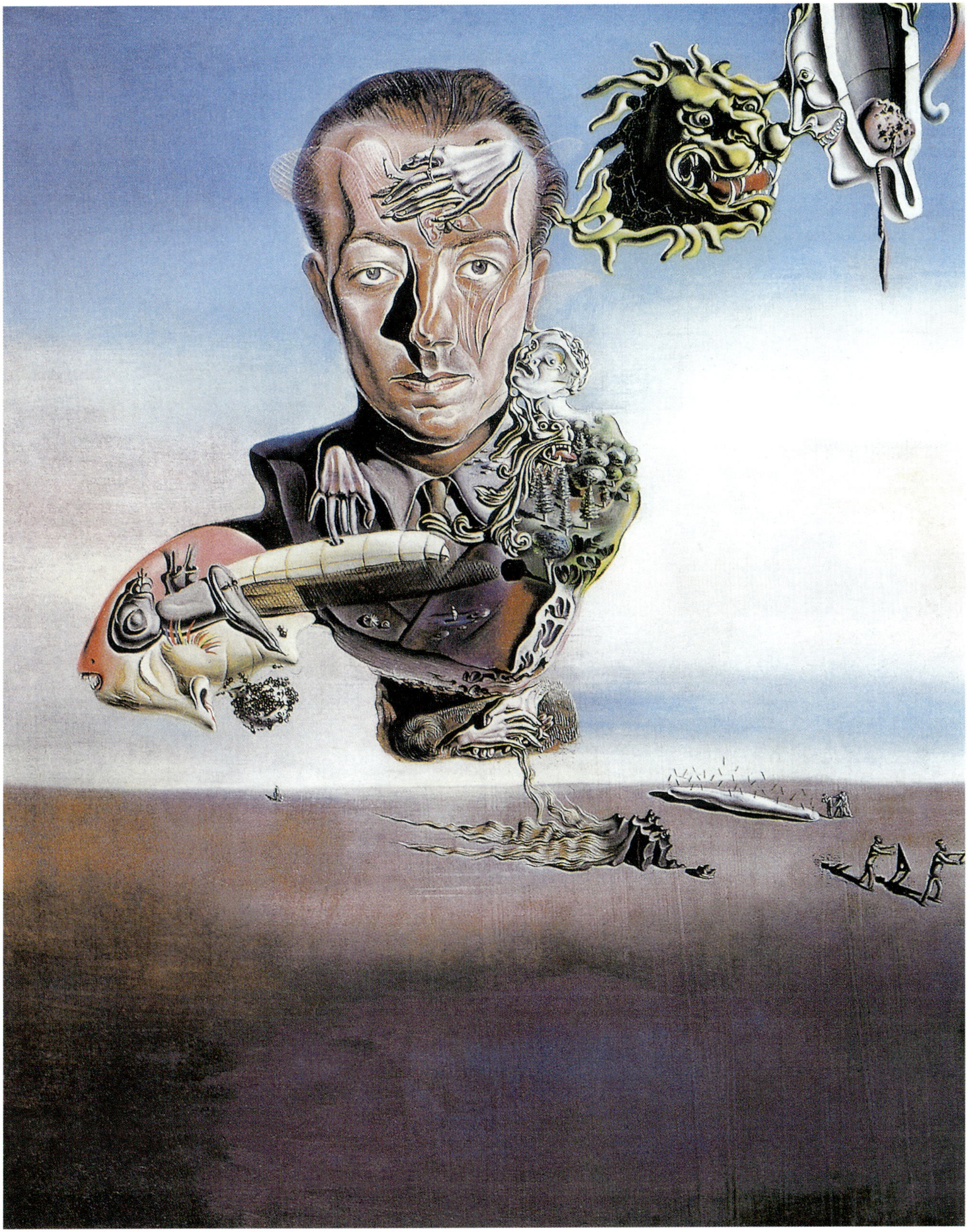

The Cut Eye. Dalí and Buñuel

Dalí's friendship with Buñuel preceded that with Garcia Lorca; it was only after Buñuel moved to Paris in 1925 that Dalí drew close to Lorca. Already in Madrid, Dalí and Buñuel forged plans for a joint film project. However, this only took on real shape in the summer of 1928, when Buñuel visited Dalí in Figueras. Six months later they met once more to finish the script, which they gave the title *Un Chien andalou* – An Andalusian Dog. Later, both authors claimed the central ideas in this joint project as their own. Dalí even claimed to be singularly responsible for the whole scenario: "His [Buñuel's] film idea appeared to me to be extremely average, it was of an unbelievable naive avant-garde nature. I told Buñuel that his film story did not excite the least interest. However, I, in comparison, had just written a very short script which incorporated a touch of the brilliant and which was the exact counterpart of the present film."[17]

Some motifs in the film could already be found in the earlier paintings and writings of Dalí. At the end of 1926, he began working on the painting *Honey is Sweeter than Blood*: the body of a naked woman can be seen on a beach with hands, feet and head lying severed: the head of Garcia Lorca lying beside it with a decomposing donkey carcass. The donkey cadaver serves as a central theme in *Un Chien andalou*, and the scene where the woman's pupil is cut with a razor is regarded as the most well known sequence. The cut eye became a central image for the Surrealists. In the spring of 1929, Dalí travelled to Paris to see the film being shot. The painter also used his stay in the French capital to look after his business affairs. There he signed a contract with the gallerist Camille Goemans and Joan Miró, who Dalí had met by way of a family friend, introduced his fellow countryman to the various Parisian circles. Dalí encountered the painter René Magritte, the sculptor Hans Arp, and the poet Paul Éluard. In a private screening on June 6th, 1929, *Un Chien andalou* was shown for the first time at the Studio des Ursulines. The audience responded to it in the way that Dalí had expected and hoped: "I wanted [the film] to shock and disrupt the normal attitudes of thought as well as the viewing attitudes and the taste that the intellectuals and snobs of the capital had for petit-bougeois entertainment; a film which was designed to return each viewer to the secret realm of their childhood"[18]

Following *Un Chien andalou*, Buñuel and Dalí became firmly placed in the spotlight of Parisian cultural life. The Viscount Charles de Noailles and his wife Marie-Laure suggested to the two Spaniards that they make another film, this time in feature-length and with sound. The noble couple were prepared to cover the production costs.

25. ***Partial Hallucination. Six apparitions of Lenin on a Grand Piano***, 1931. Oil on canvas. 114 x 146 cm. The National Museum of Modern Art, Georges Pompidou Centre, Paris.

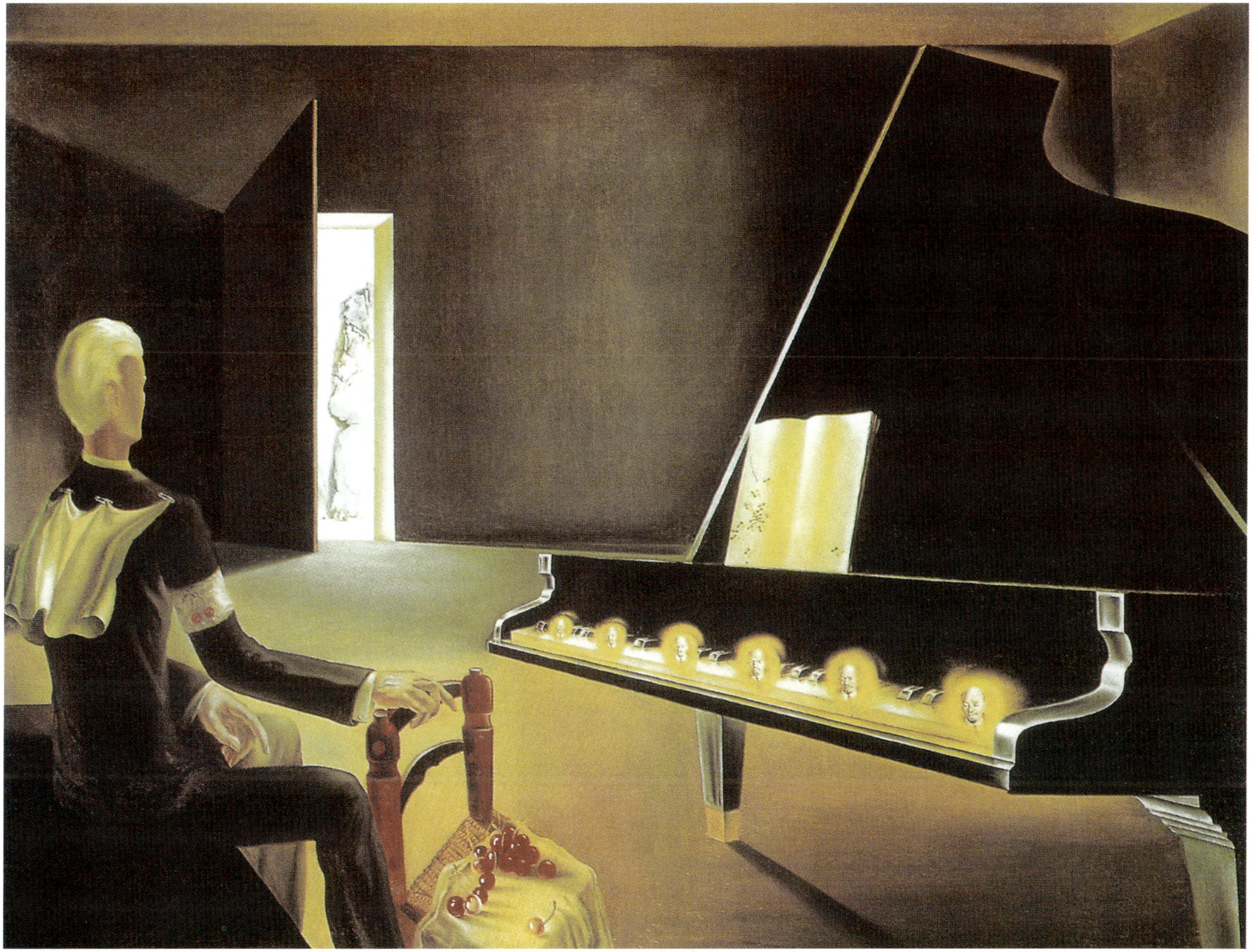

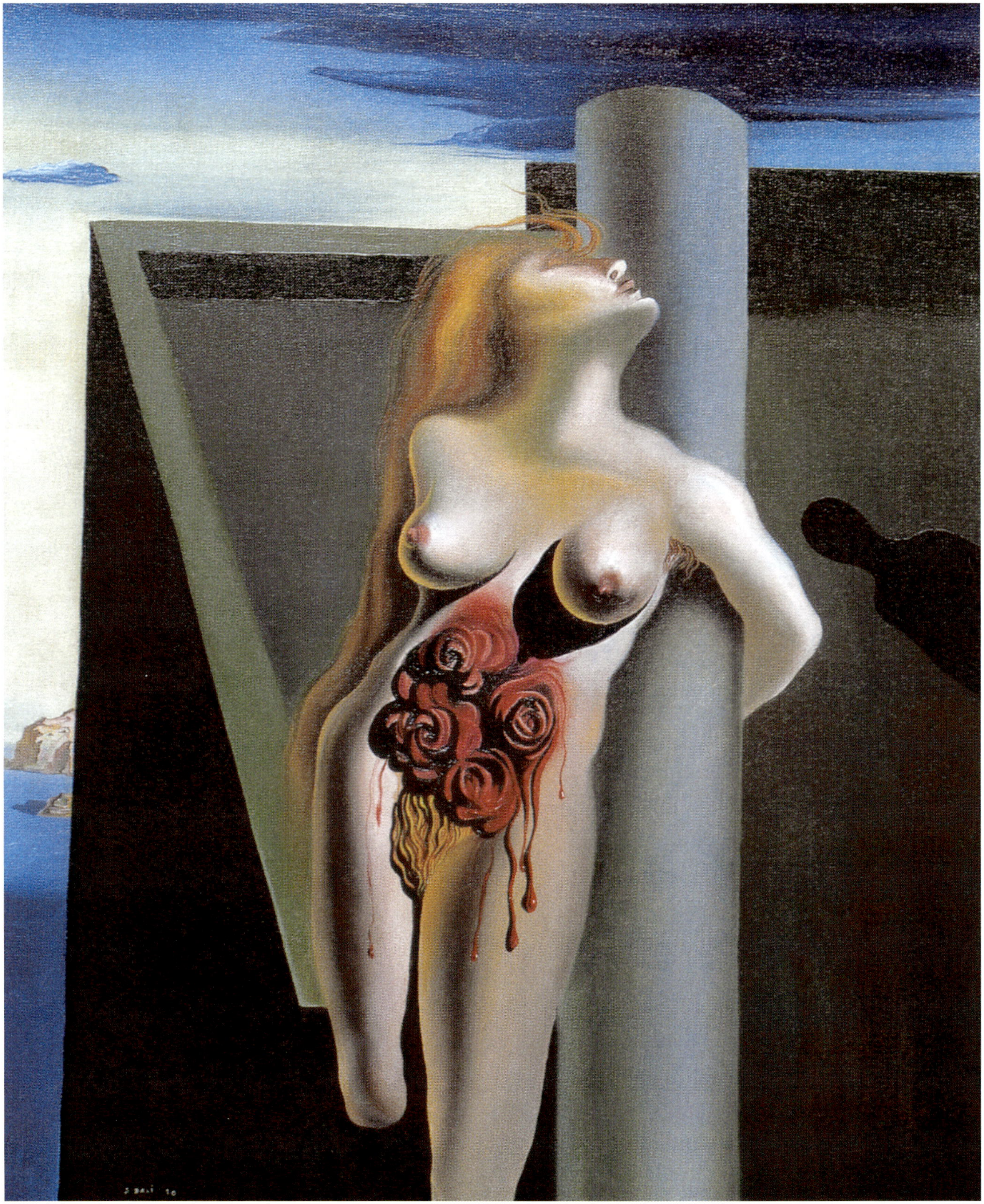

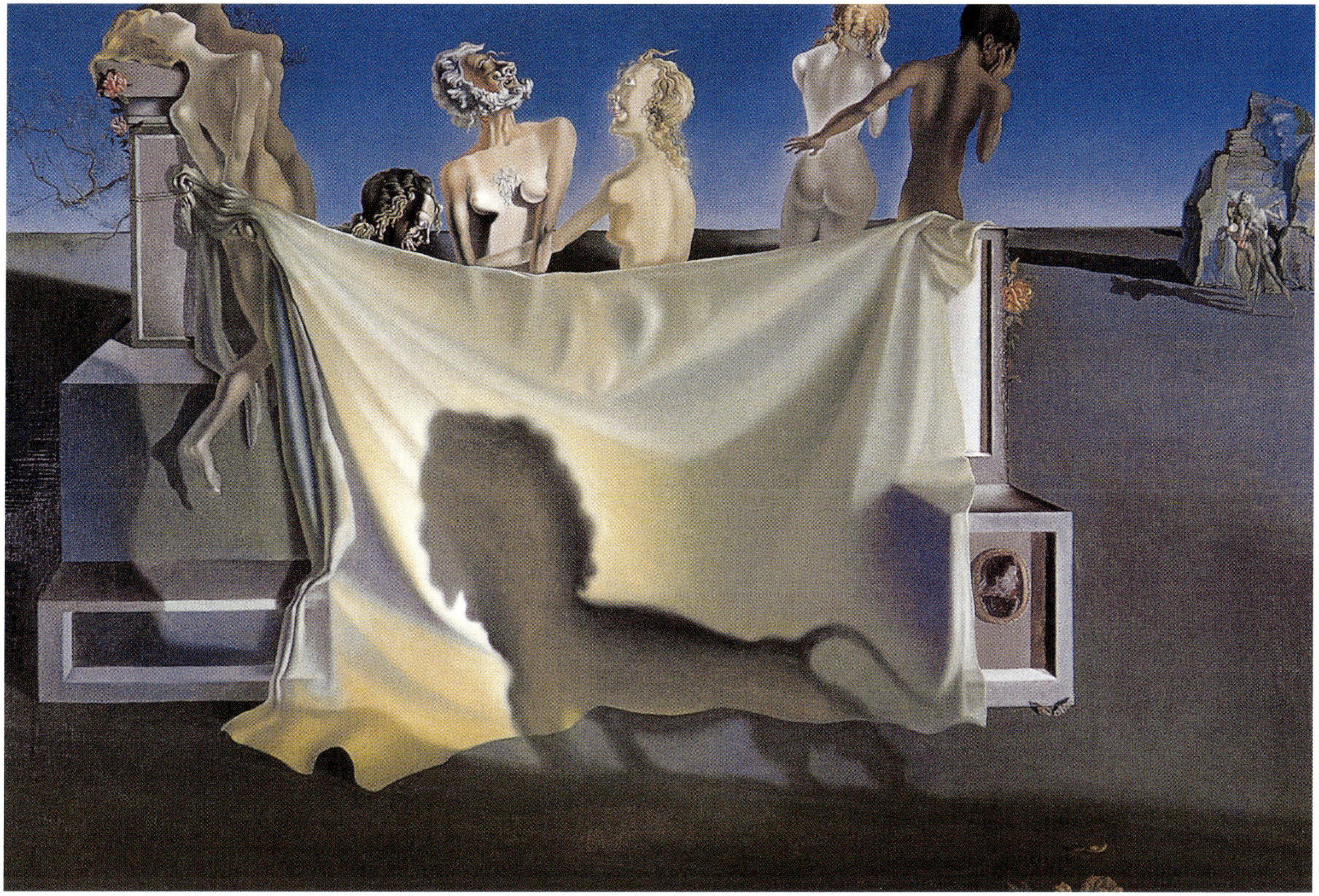

The title of the project changed several times but the name, *L'âge d'or – The Golden Age*, was finally agreed upon. For Dalí, the period between both films is characterised by several events and changes of a decisive and radical nature. In the summer of 1929, he met Gala Éluard in Cadaqués and they fell in love with one another. At the end of November, shortly before Buñuel was due to visit Figueras, a dispute broke out between Dalí and his father. Dalí traveled to Cadaqués. A few days later, his father told him the family wished to have nothing more to do with him. One reason for his father's anger may have been Dalí's relationship with Gala, who at this time was still married to Paul Éluard. A further cause may have been Dalí's ink-drawing *The Sacred Heart*. On it, Dalí had written: "Sometimes, I spit on the portrait of my mother for fun". At the same time in Paris, Buñuel began filming *The Golden Age*.

26. ***The Bleeding Roses***, 1930. Oil on canvas. 75 x 64 cm. Private collection, Geneva.

27. ***The Old Age of William Tell***, 1931. Oil on canvas. 98 x 140 cm. Private collection.

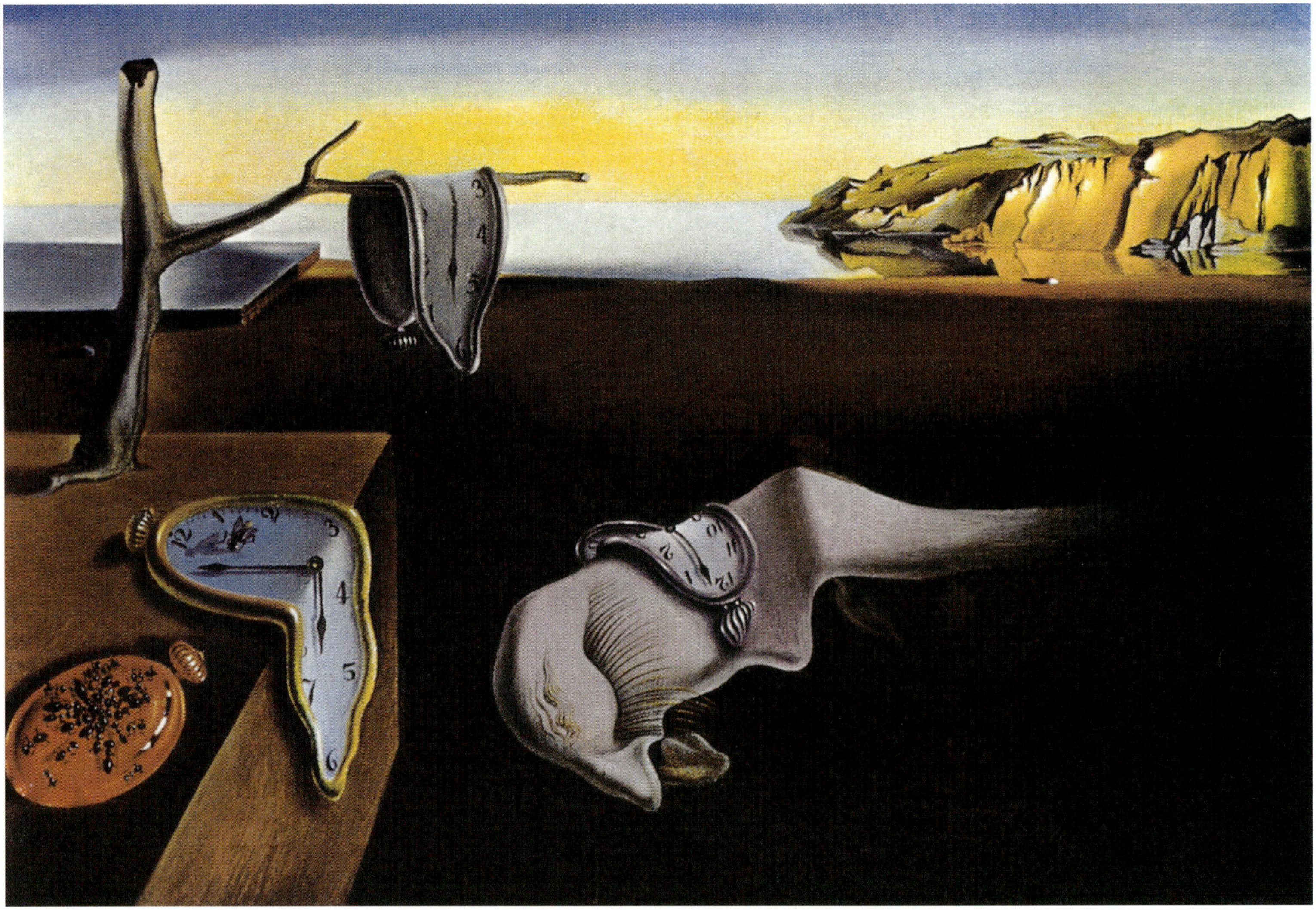

28. ***The Persistance of Memory***, 1931. Oil on canvas. 24 x 33 cm. Museum of Modern Art, New York.

29. ***Fried Eggs on the Plate without the Plate***, 1932. Oil on canvas. 60 x 42 cm. The Salvador Dali Museum, St Petersburg.

Dalí was not present during the production of the film and did not appear in it, but instead dedicated himself to the project in thought and reported his ideas to Buñuel by letter. Not all his suggestions were taken up by his partner and when they were, they were significantly changed. In his autobiography, Dalí wrote: "Even in those days I was moved and intoxicated, yes even possessed by the magnificence and splendor of Catholicism. I said to Buñuel: "For this film I want plenty of archbishops, mortal remains and monstrances. I especially want archbishops, bathing between the fallen rocks at Cape Creus with their embroidered mitres. In his naïvety, and with his stubborn Aragonic manner, Buñuel managed to change all this into an example of simple anticlericalism."[19]

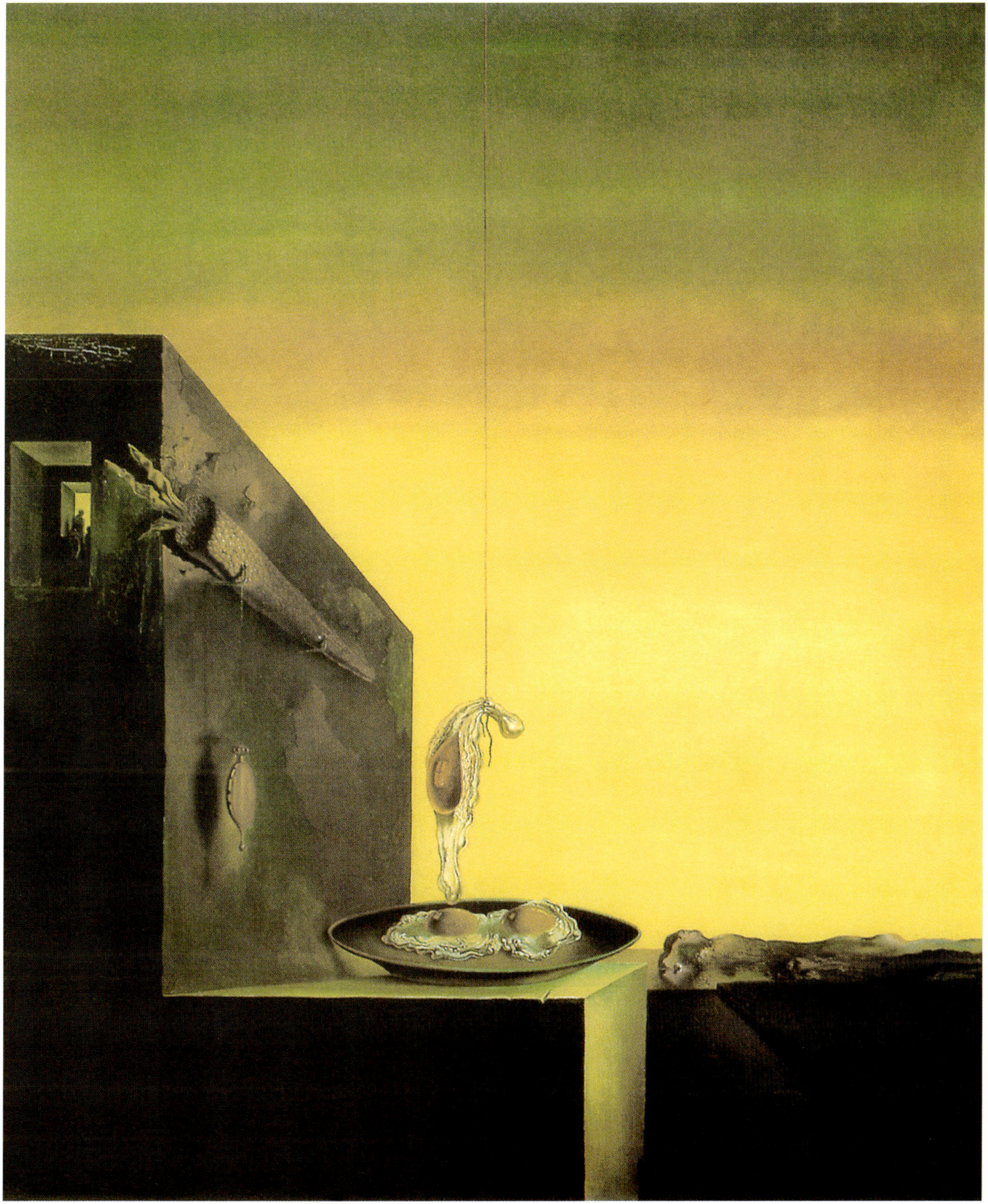

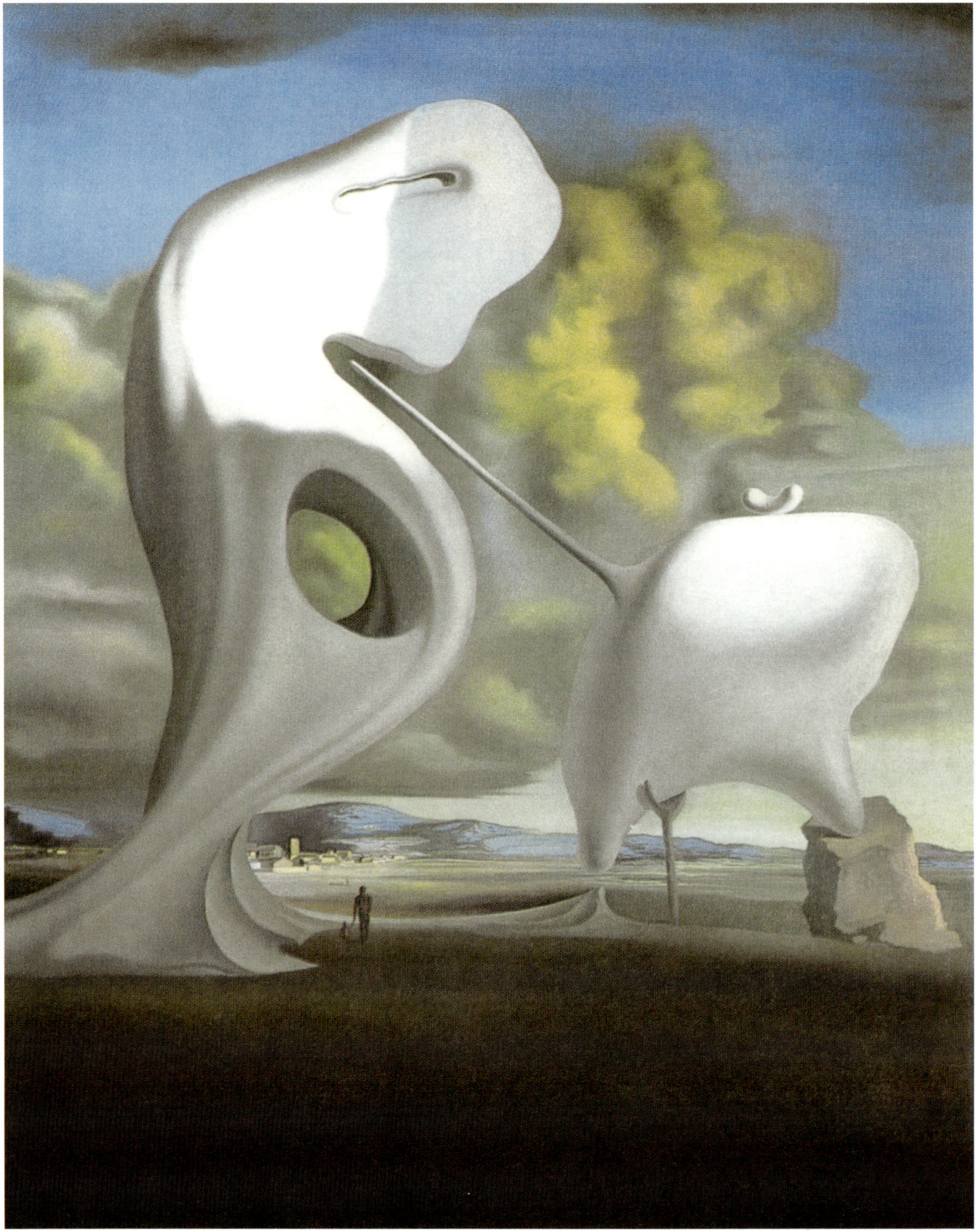

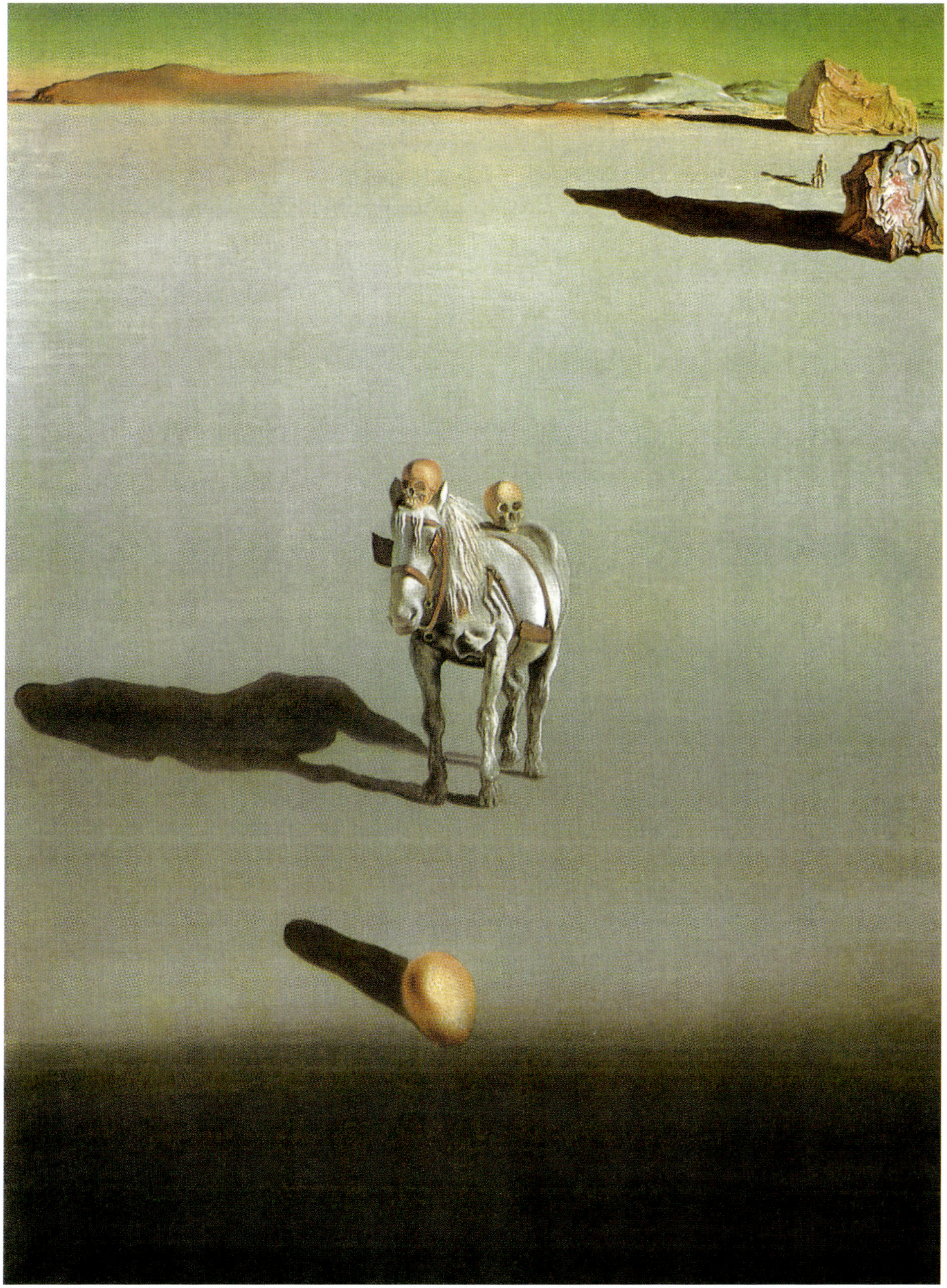

30. ***The Architectonic Angelus of Millet***, 1933. Oil on canvas. 73 x 61 cm. The Reina Sofía National Museum, Madrid.

31. ***Geological Destiny***, 1933. Oil on panel. 21 x 16 cm. Private collection.

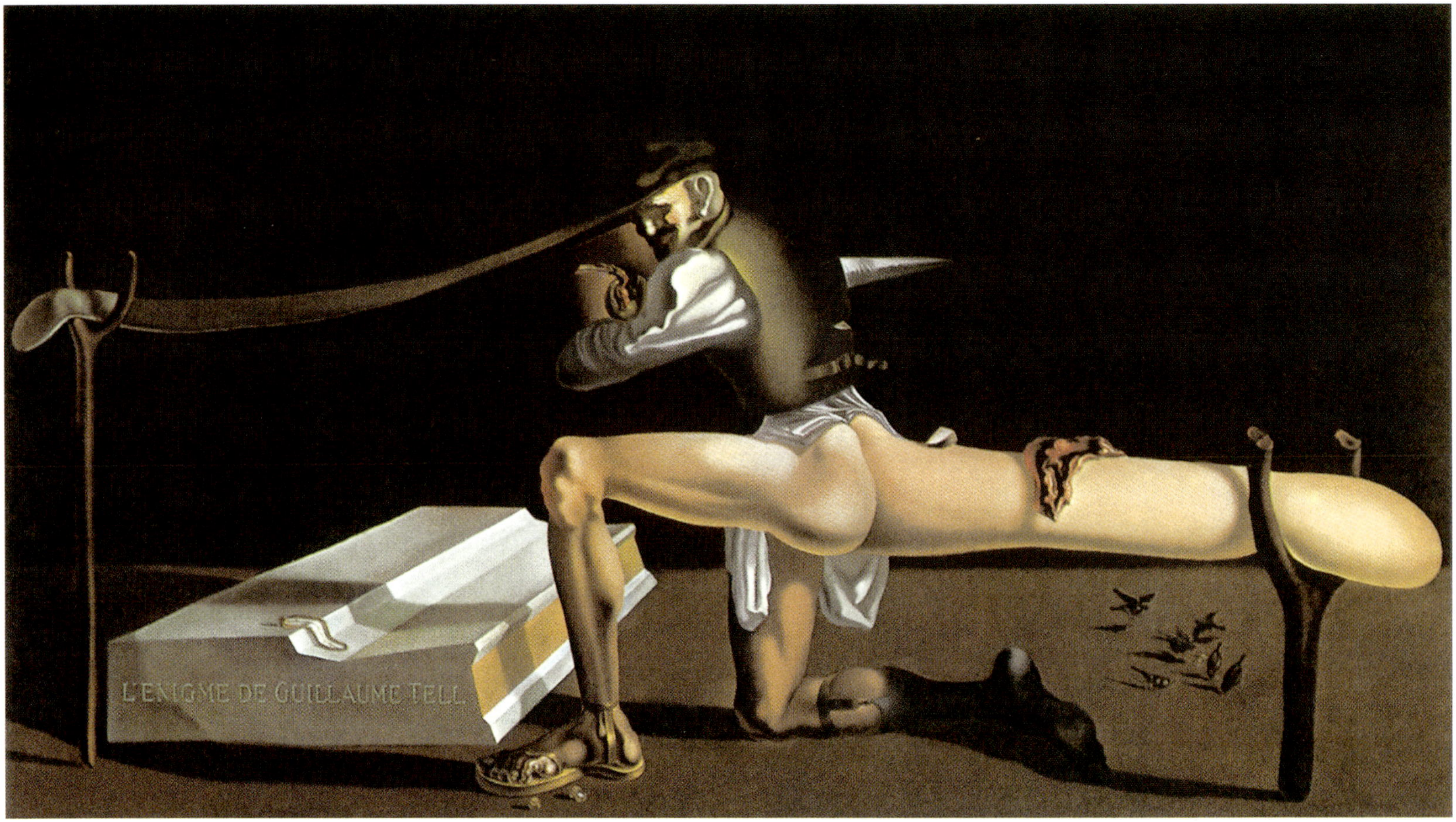

32. ***The Enigma of William Tell***, 1933. Oil on canvas. 201.5 x 346 cm. Museum of Modern Art, Stockholm.

At a private screening, *The Golden Age* was presented to a discerning audience on October 22nd, 1930. Among others, Gertrude Stein, Pablo Picasso, Marcel Duchamp, André Malraux and Man Ray were invited. The reaction to the film was extremely cool; most guests left the cinema directly after the end of the showing. On November 28th, public screenings began at Studio 28. The Parisian Surrealists took part in the event. On December 3rd, the cinema was attacked by members of the Action Française, a right-wing and antisemitic association. Apparently, the attack was not only directed against the film but also against its Jewish producer, Marie-Laure de Noailles. A week after the raid – during which most of the exhibited Surrealist paintings had been damaged – *The Golden Age* was prohibited in France. The film could not be shown for fifty years. Out of solidarity to Buñuel but not out of conviction, Dalí defended the film: "I accepted responsibility for the sacrilegious scandal, although I did not have any ambition in that direction."[20] The friendship had however hit rocky ground.

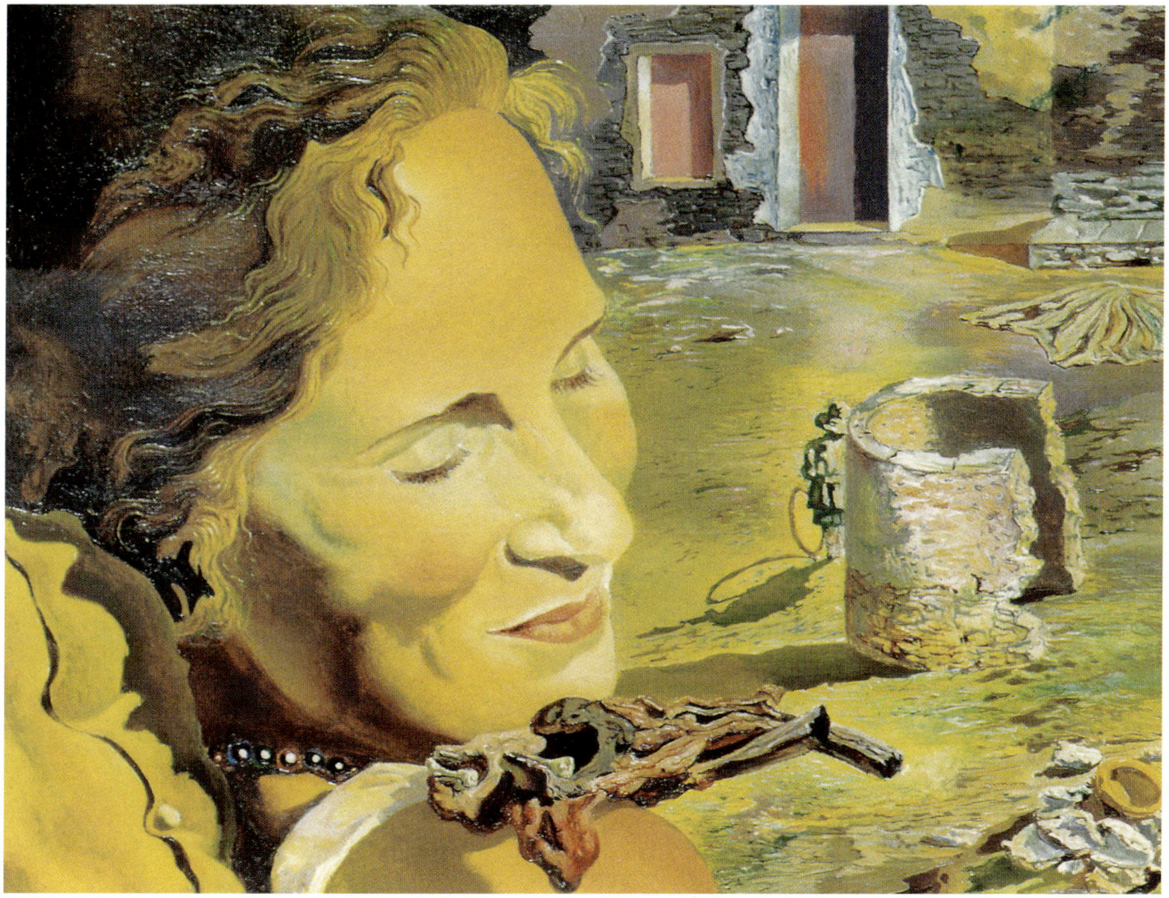

The final break came in 1934. Dalí had seen a new version of *Un Chien andalou* and had noticed that his name was no longer mentioned. In Barcelona at the same time, *The Golden Age* was being announced as a "Film from Buñuel, in cooperation with Dalí" and not as a work of equal parts between Buñuel and Dalí. The director rejected his friend's claim. Over the course of the following years, in various interviews, they both never tired of making repeated reference to the role that each played in the authorship of the piece.

Gala: or The Healing Gradiva. The Surrealist Years in Paris

In the summer of 1929, the gallerist Camille Goemans visited Dalí in Cadaqués with René Magritte, Luis Buñuel and Paul Éluard. Éluard was accompanied by his wife Gala, and Dalí instantly fell in love.

33. ***Portrait of Gala with Two Lamb Chops Balanced on her Shoulder***, 1933.
Oil on olive panel.
6 x 8 cm.
The Gala-Salvador Dalí Foundation, Figueras.

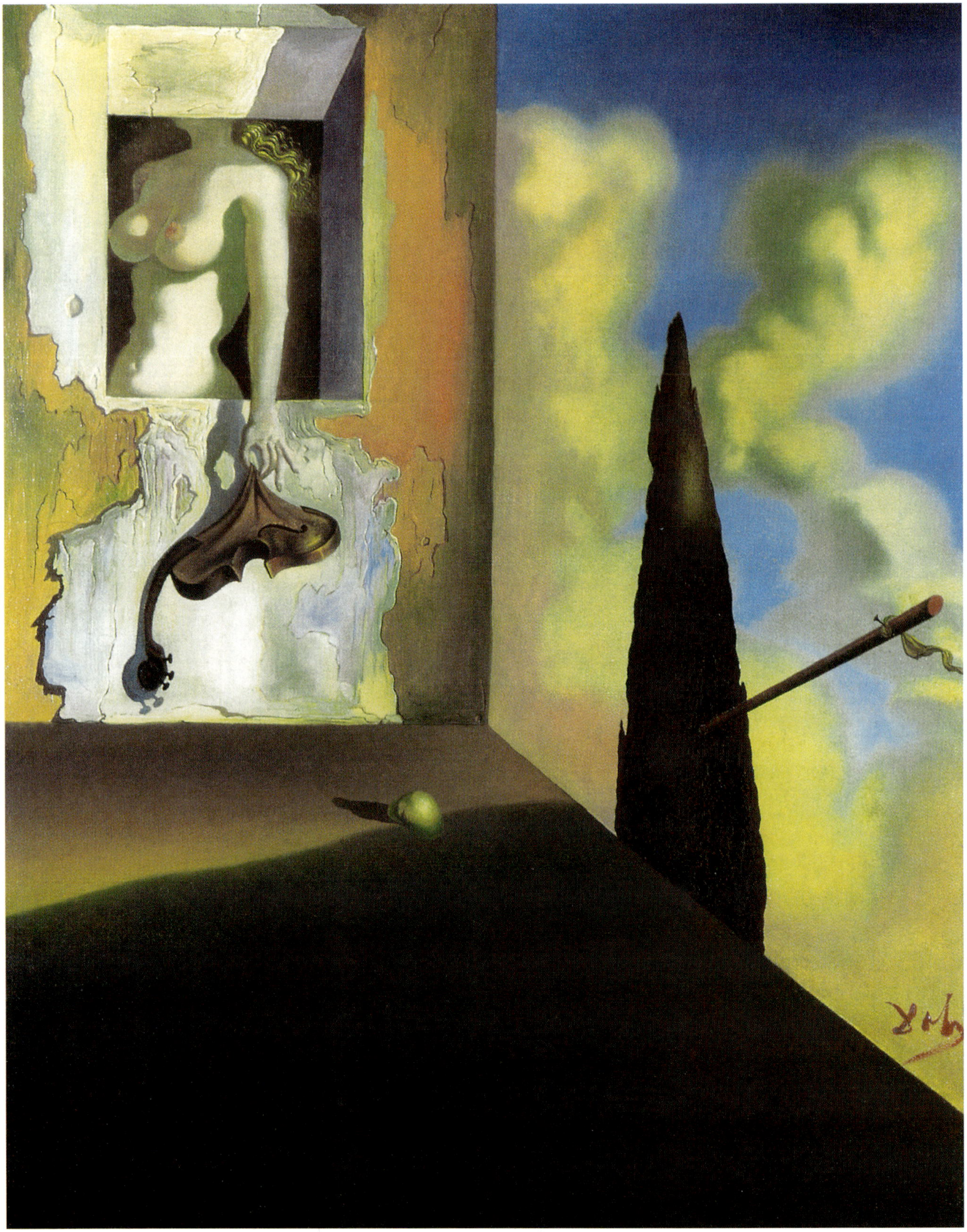

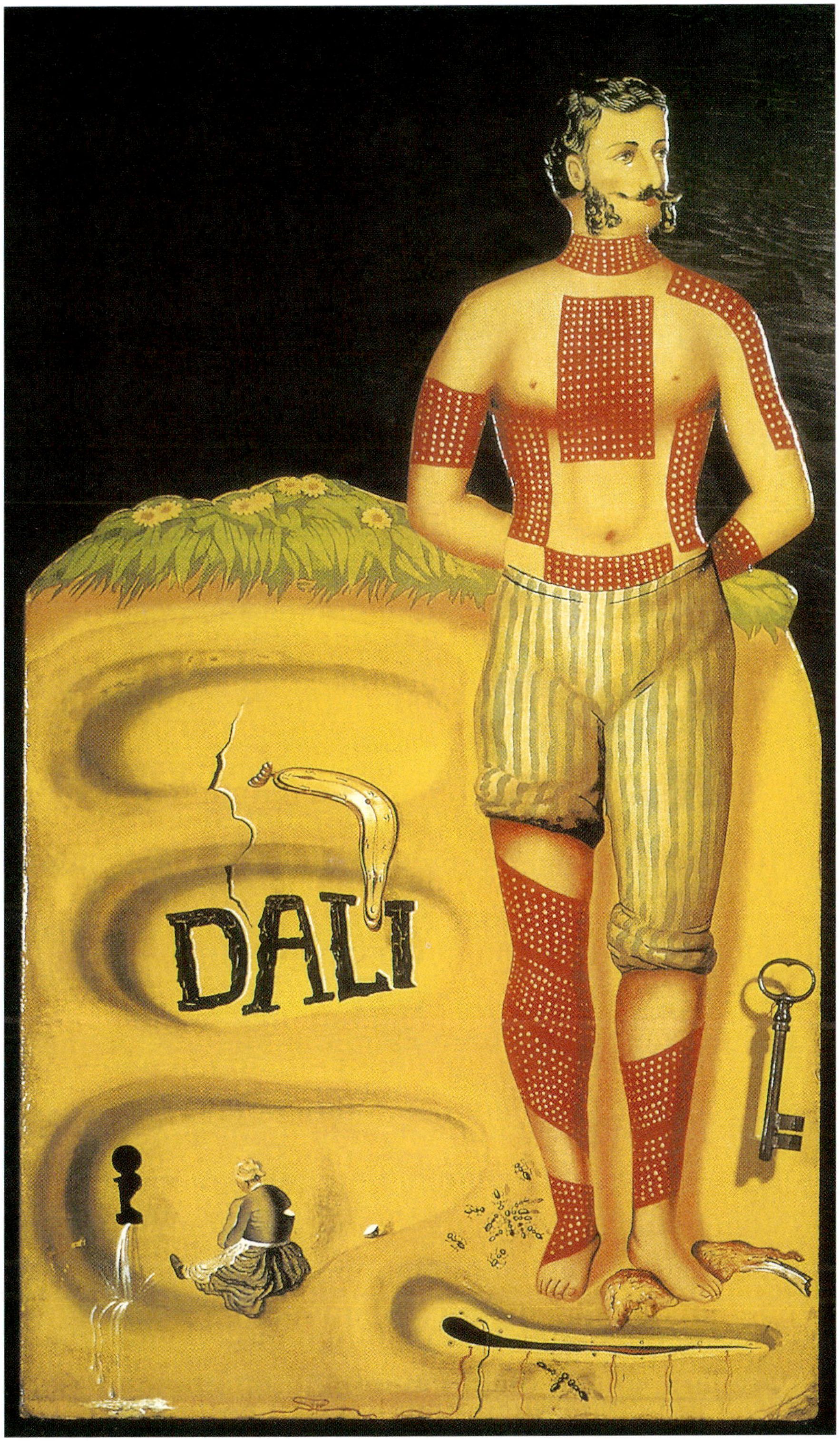

34. ***Masochist Instrument***,
1933-1934.
Oil on canvas.
62 x 47 cm.
Private collection.

35. ***Surrealist Poster***,
1934. Oil on
chromolithographic
advertising poster
with key. 69 x 46 cm.
The Salvador Dalí
Museum,
St Petersburg (FL).

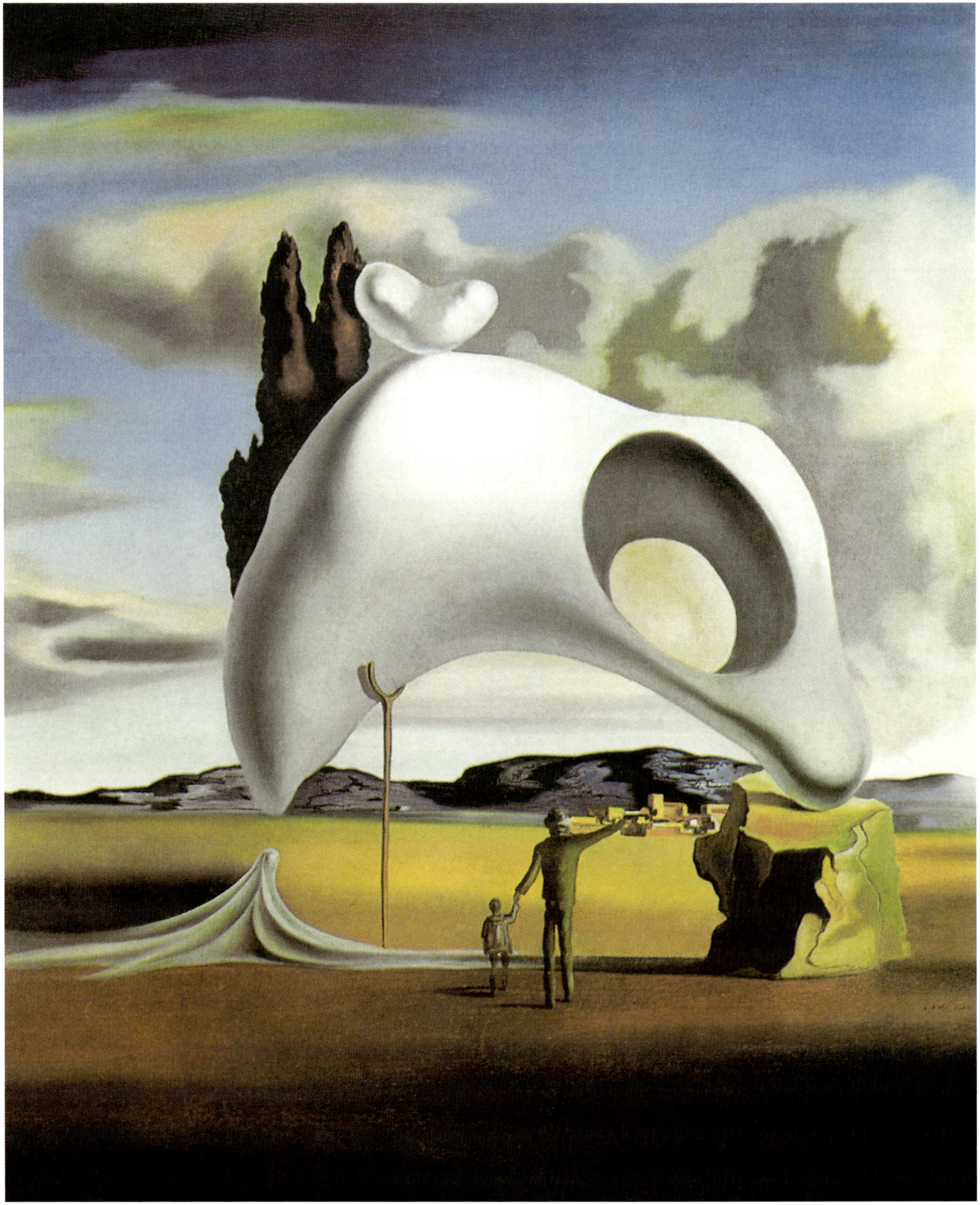

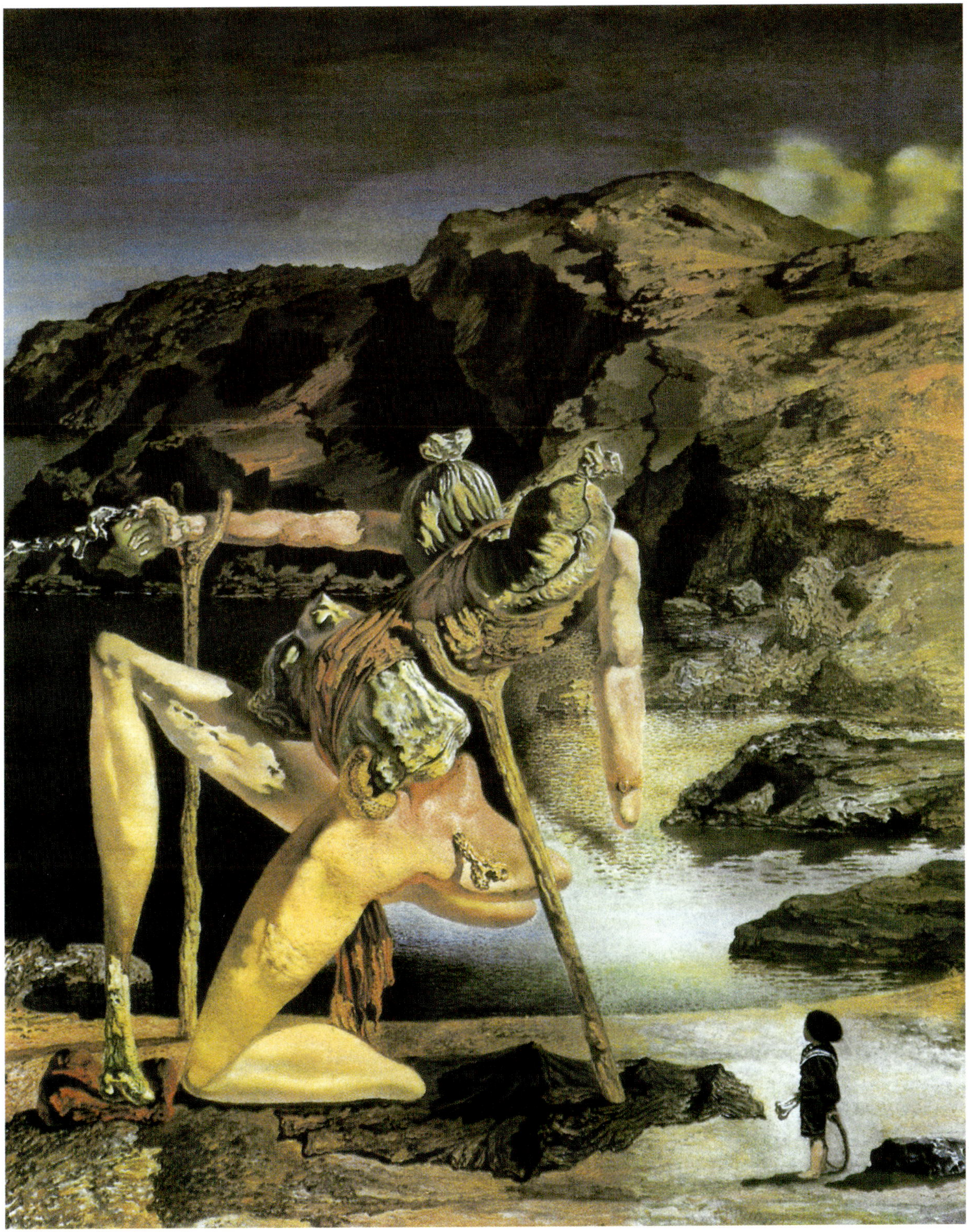

36. ***Atavistic Vestiges After the Rain***, 1934.
Oil on canvas.
65 x 54 cm.
Perls Galleries,
New York.

37. ***The Spectre of Sex Appeal***, 1934.
Oil on panel.
18 x 14 cm.
The Gala-Salvador Dalí Foundation,
Figueras.

Éluard had affairs with other women and also wished that his own wife would live out her passions with other men. Between 1921 and 1924, the painter Max Ernst lived with the couple, and was at this time also Gala's lover. Many Surrealists paid court to the beautiful Mrs Éluard. André Breton called her "the eternal woman". As Gala fell in love with Dalí in 1929, Éluard considered it just a brief love affair. He was deceived: Gala separated from him. She remained at Dalí's side until her death in 1982, marrying him at a church wedding in 1956, four years after Éluard's death. Dalí continually stressed that he would never have become the Dalí that he was without this woman at his side. For him she was muse, model, and manager all in one. She organized Dalí's business affairs because, as he confessed, he let everybody cheat him while Gala always saw through their plans.[21] He honoured her importance for his artistic work by signing many of his paintings with "Gala Salvador Dalí". Furthermore, Gala freed him of his impotence complex, something that had paralysed him since his early youth. On the one hand, Dalí traced his fear of sexuality back to his father, who had often elaborated on the dangers of venereal disease to him as a child, and, on the other, to his reading of books that portrayed sadomasochistic games, which he wrongly understood to be depictions of the real act of love: "At that time my libido degenerated into such a state of downright erotic idiocy as a result of this impotence-complex [...] I dressed myself as a king and masturbated and had I not found Gala, who helped me discover, so to speak, normal love, then it would have taken no more than two years for all my hallucinations to over-step the measure of paranoia to such an extent that they would have become psychopathological."[22] A painting that Dalí began in the autumn of 1929 carries the title *The Great Masturbator*. Several other works painted in this year also concern themselves with the head of the "Masturbator". In *Puzzle of Desire*, a honeycomb structure grows out of it and in its various chambers "*ma mère*" – "my mother" – is written. It also forms the central focus in *The Dark Game* and *Inspired Pleasures*. The four paintings were shown at Dalí's first single exhibition in Paris, at the Goemans gallery at the end of November of 1929. *The Dark Game* was bought by the Viscount de Noailles, and, of all the paintings of this period, won the greatest admiration. Dalí was celebrated by the Surrealists as being one of their own, but not without reservations. In the song of praise André Breton sung about Dalí, soft tones of misgiving can be heard. The question regarding faeces became Dalí's point of test for the Surrealists: "I possessed the ideal method of and potential for communication. Very soon however, Breton became shocked by the evidence of so many obscene elements. He wanted neither excrement nor Madonna images. It defeats the very reason for having pure automatism if a system of control is introduced, for these images of excrement came to me in a direct, biological way."[23]

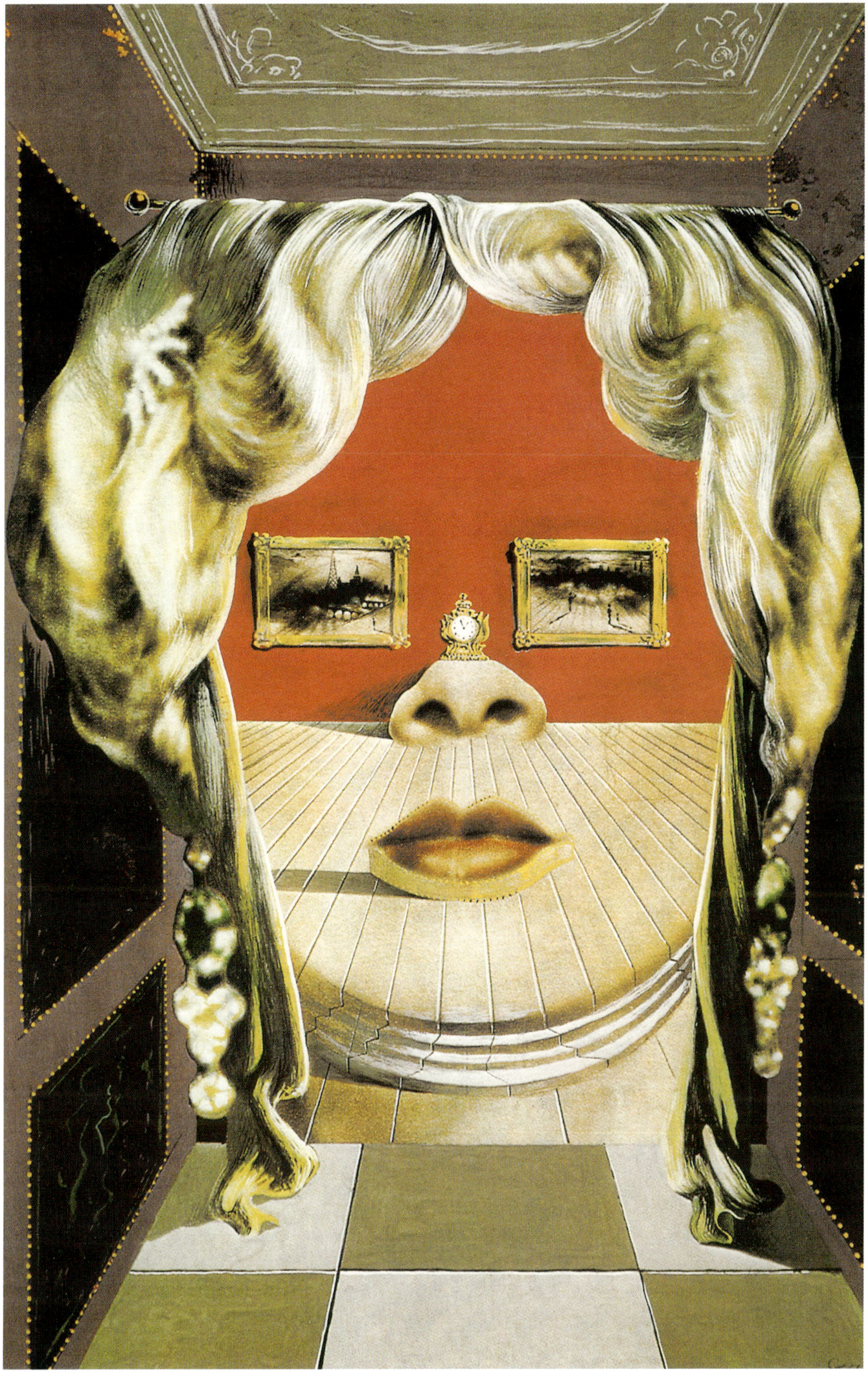

38. ***Mae West's Face which May Be Used as a Surrealist Appartment***, 1934-1935. Gouache on newspaper. 31 x 17 cm. The Art Institute of Chicago, Chicago.

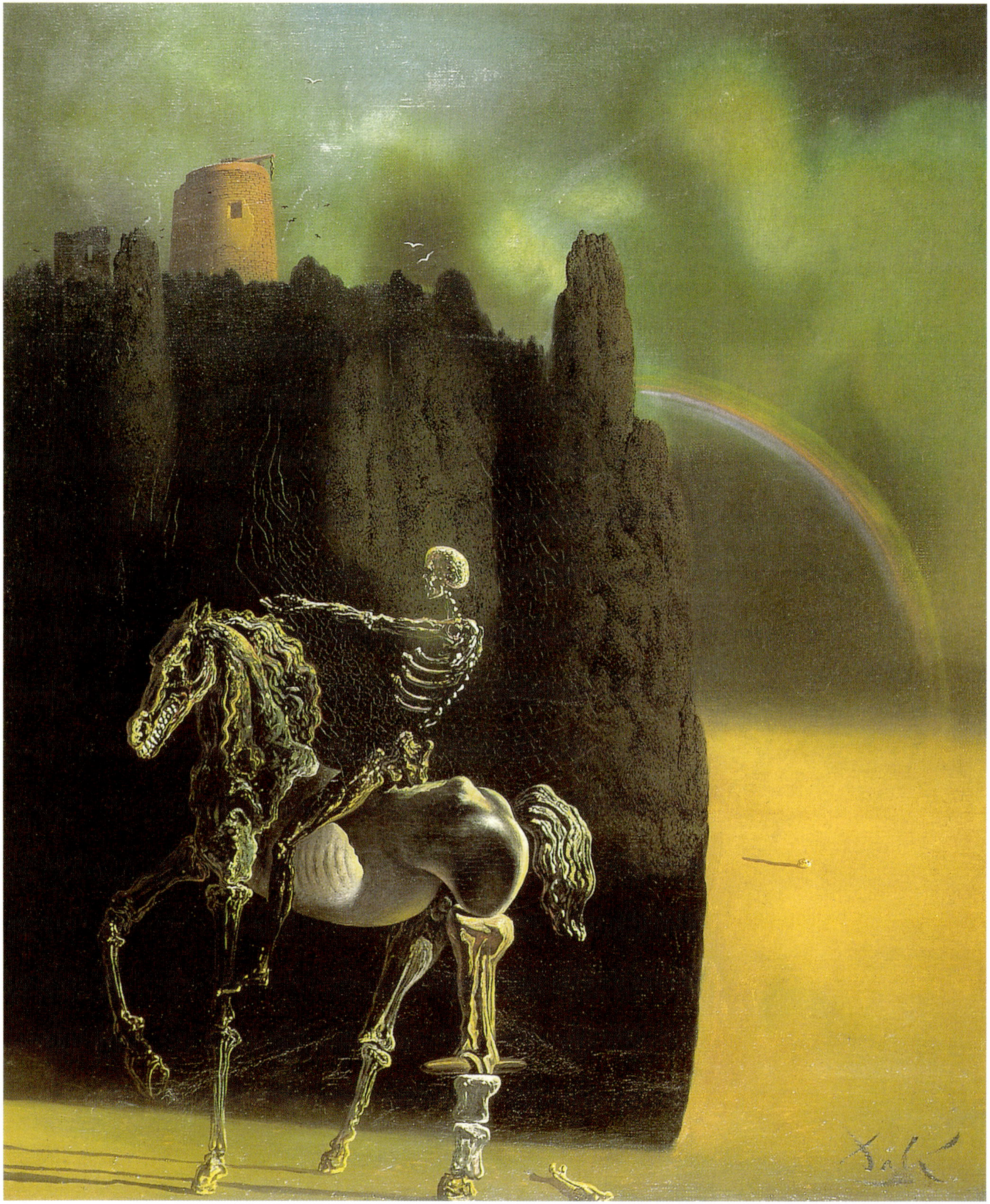

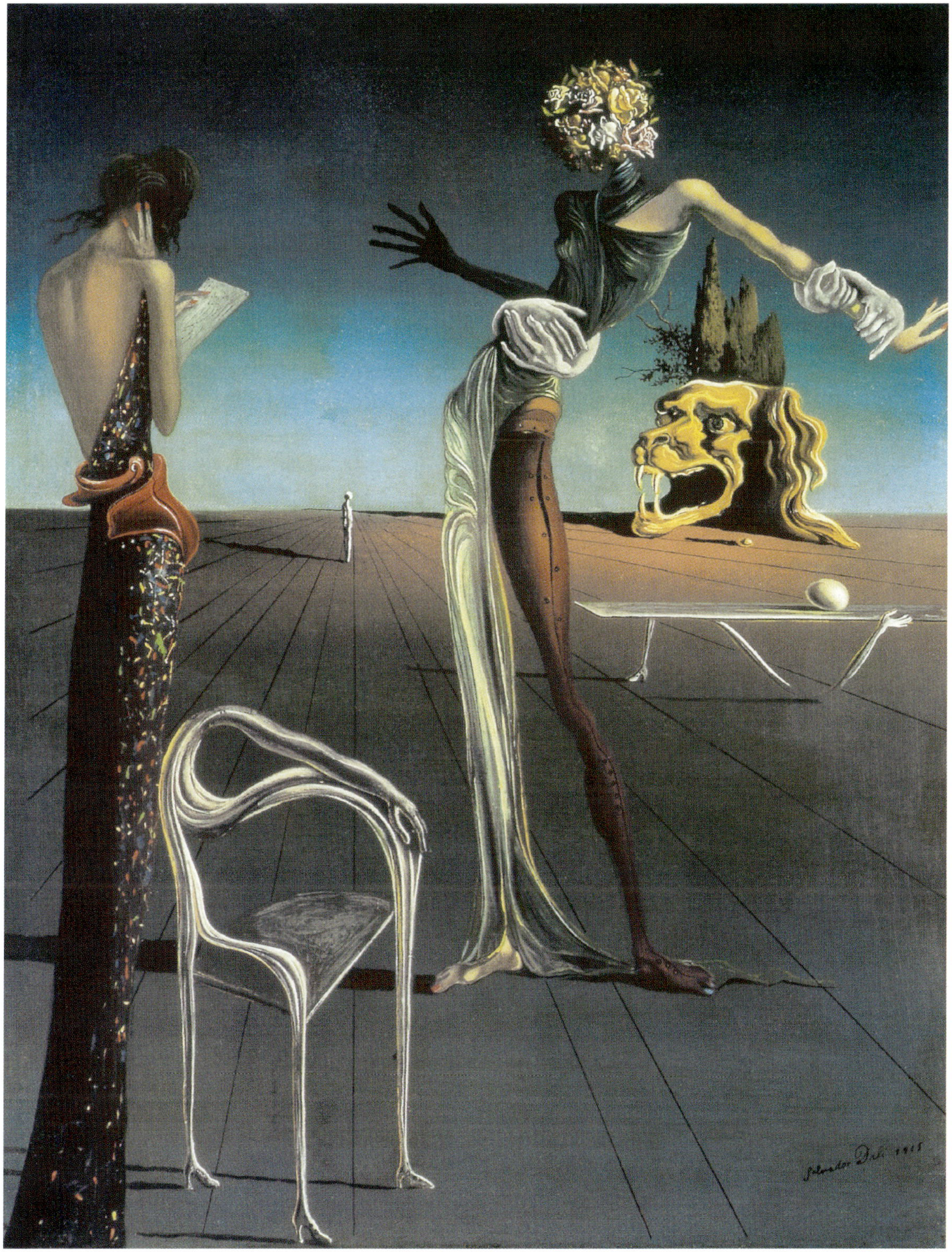

39. ***The Horseman of Death***, 1935.
Oil on canvas.
54 x 64 cm.
The André-François Petit Collection, Paris.

40. ***Woman with a Head of Roses***, 1935.
Oil on panel.
35 x 27 cm.
Kunsthaus Zürich, Zürich.

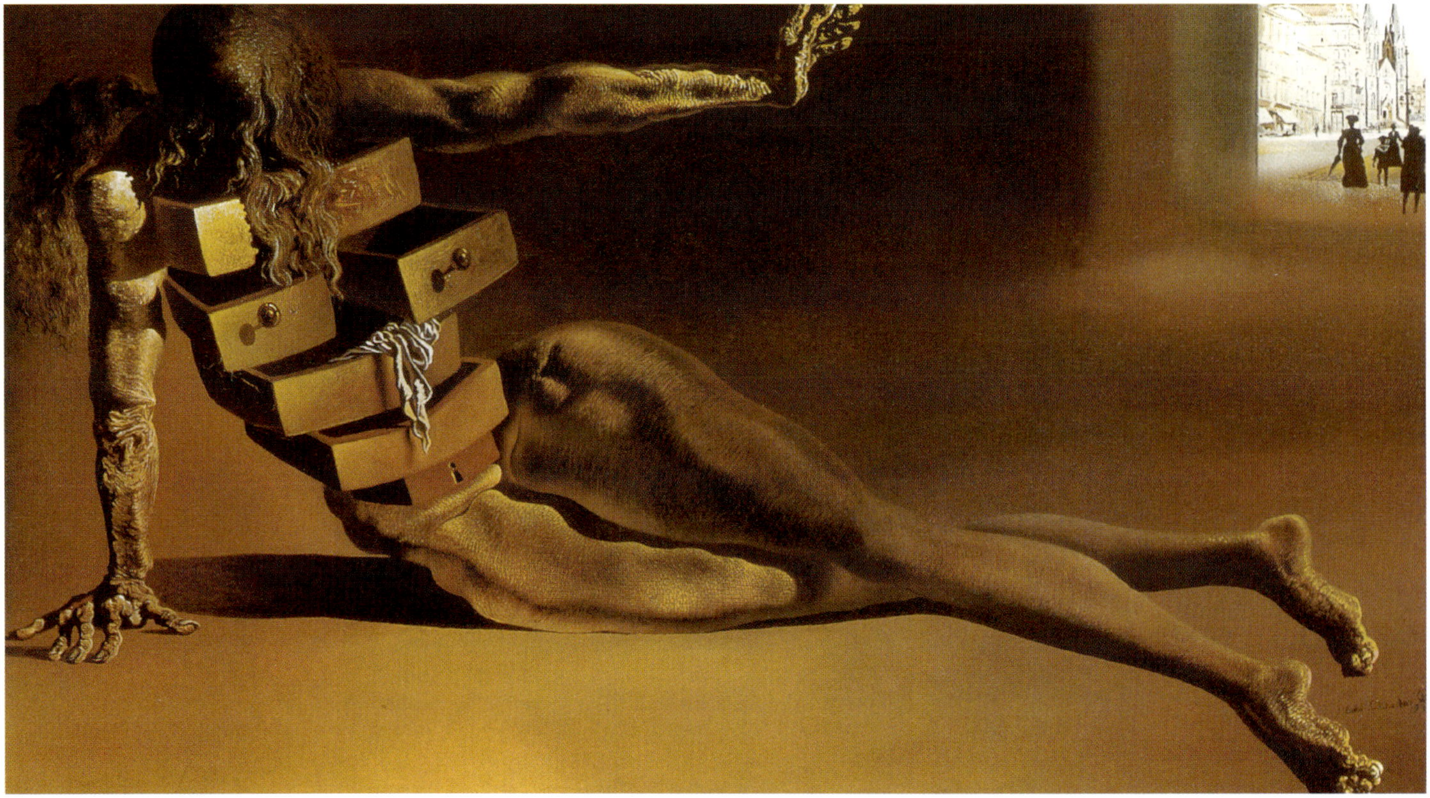

41. ***The Anthropomorphic Cabinet***, 1936.
Oil on panel.
25.4 x 44.2 cm.
Kunstsammlung Nordrhein-Westfalen, Düsseldorf.

42. ***Soft Construction with Boiled Beans – Premonition of Civil War***, 1936.
Oil on canvas.
100 x 99 cm.
The Philadelphia Museum of Art, Philadelphia.

From the very beginning, Dalí took on the position of outsider in the Parisian Surrealist scene. He did not just laugh about Breton's censored automatism, he also remained distant with regard to the political commitment of the group. Nevertheless, for several years, the Surrealists celebrated him as their most important representative. Dalí had, in the judgment of Breton, elevated the Surrealist mind to the point of radiance like no other before him.[24] In addition to the apparently useless Surrealist objects he used to make, Dalí also invented a series of "practical" objects such as furniture made out of Bakelite, which was supposed to adapt itself to the shape of the buyer's body, or even water-trousers as a substitute for the bathtub. Dalí hoped to be able to earn money with his original ideas, for at this time his pictures were selling badly. However, it was just as difficult to convince anybody to manufacture his inventions. Despite their permanent money troubles, Dalí always ensured that he and Gala did not have to live the life of Bohemians with their dirty sheets and continual fear that the electricity would be cut off. While living very economically within their four walls, outside the home they demonstrated that all was well by continually giving good tips. Dalí's financial situation began to improve in 1933, when a group of collectors guaranteed him the frequent purchase of his pictures.

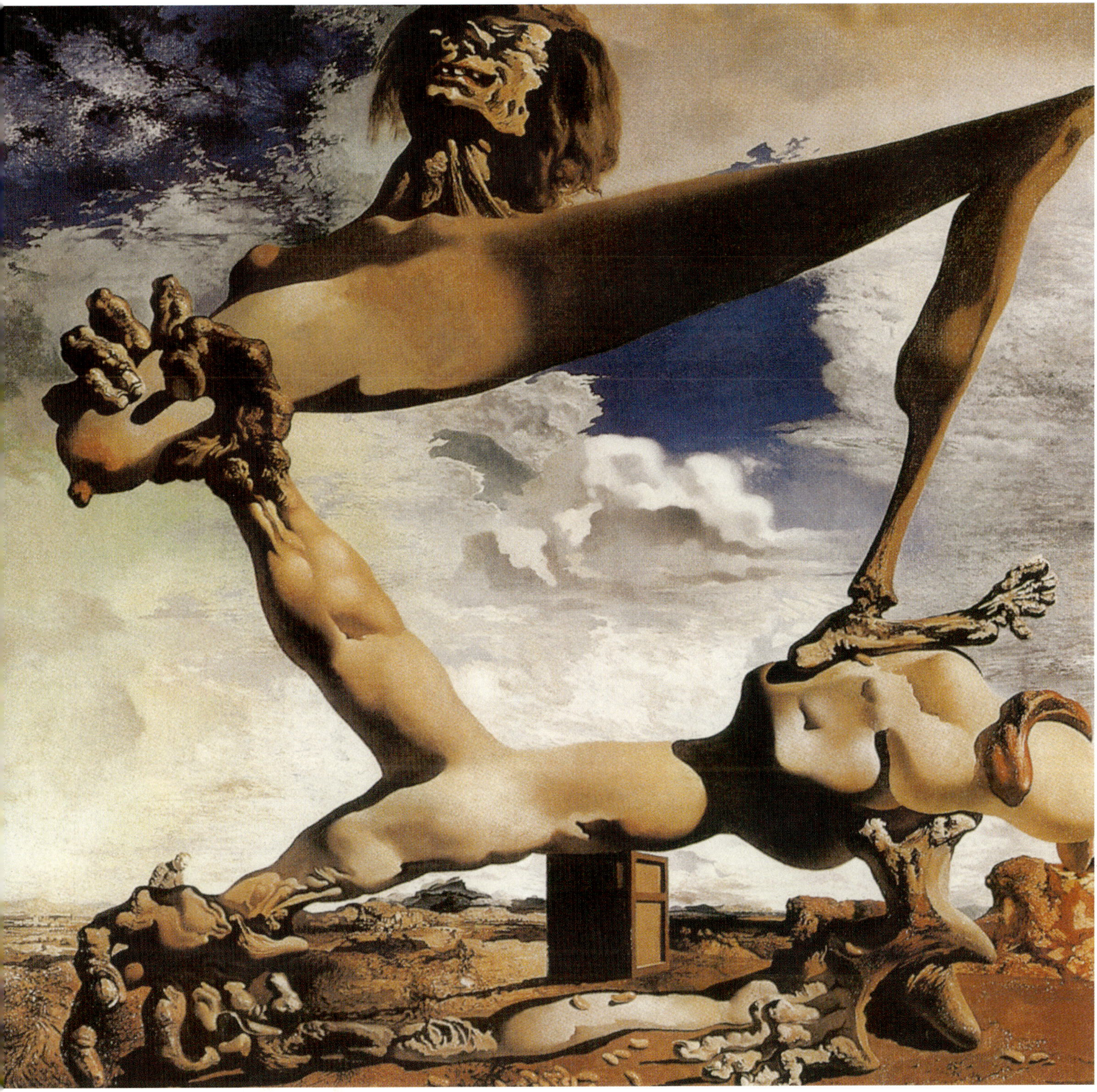

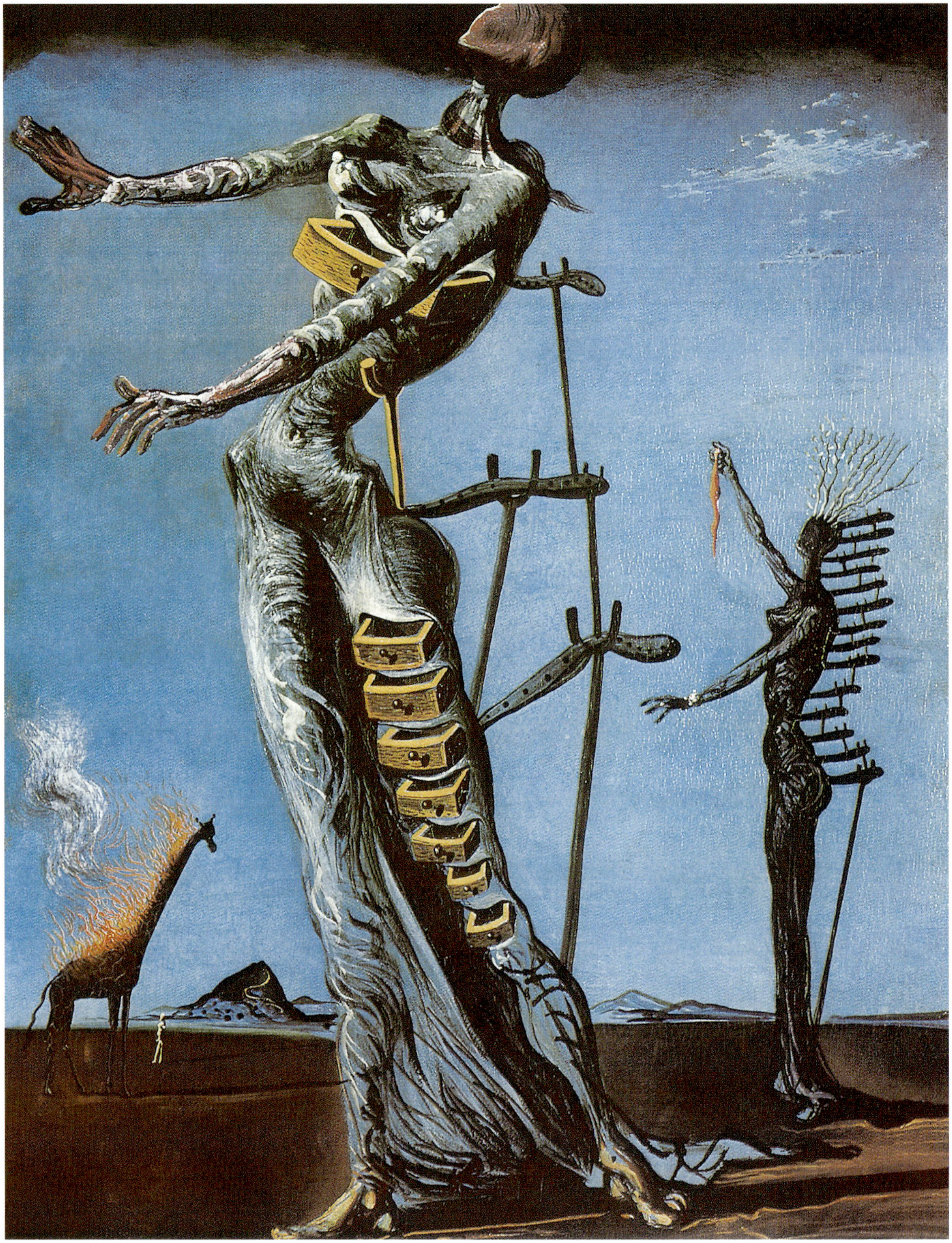

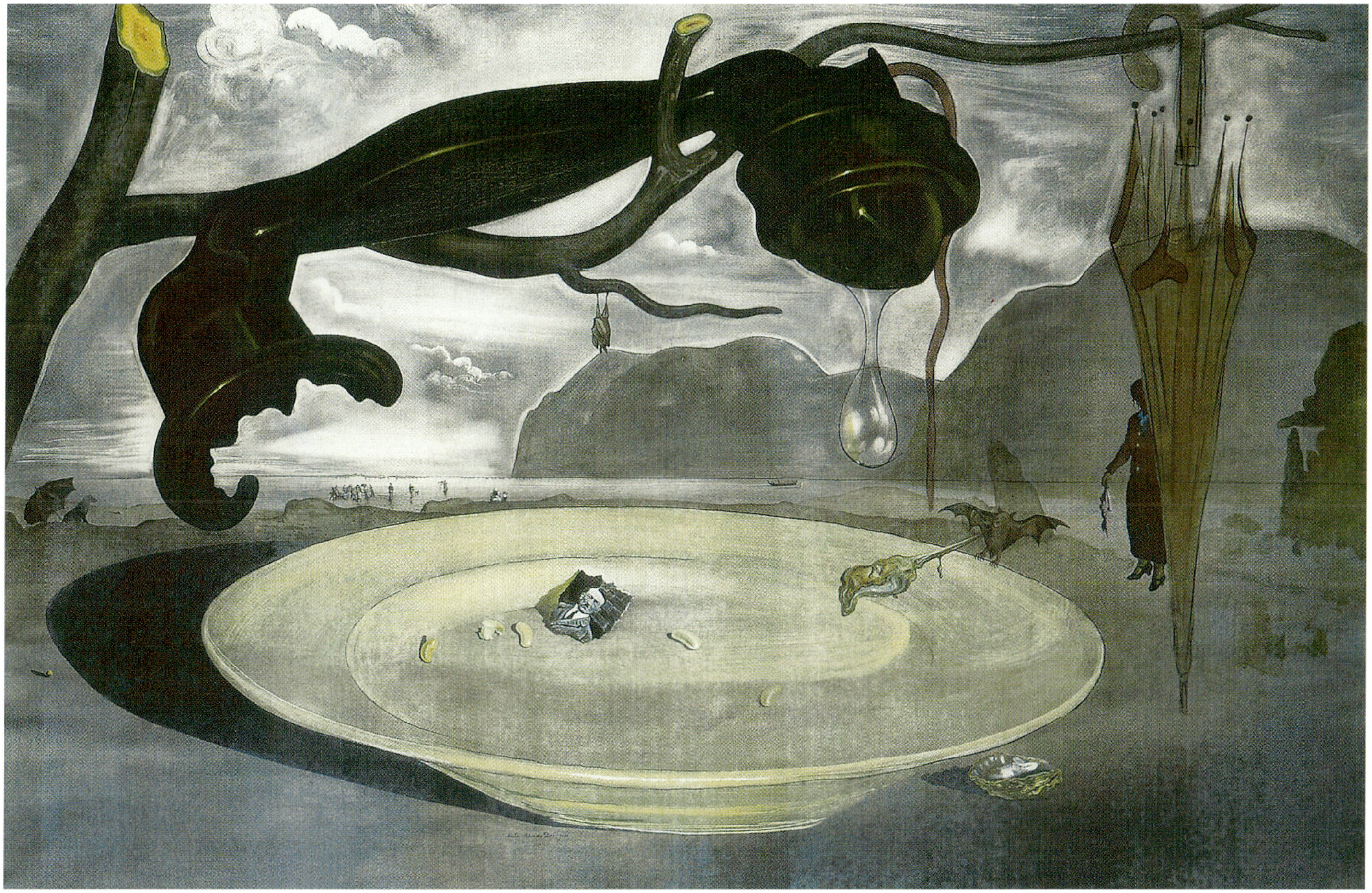

Due to his eccentric ideas, Dalí acquired a growing reputation in Paris, subsequently opening the doors to many social events: "I became indispensable at all these ultrasnobish receptions where my cane kept the beat at many successful evenings. [...] I invented artificial finger-nails made out of little mirrors, which reflected the highlights of the eyes; [...] one day I appeared with a transparent dressmakers-doll, in which red fish swam around. Every appearance was an event filled with tension."[25] Due to Dalí's political opinions, more than once disputes broke out amongst the far-reaching, Left-oriented Surrealist group. In 1933, he criticized the foreign policies of the Soviet Union and professed to be fascinated by Hitler: When Dalí exhibited his painting *The Riddle of William Tell* in the Salon of the Indépendants at the beginning of 1934, it came to a head: the picture was understood as ridiculing Lenin. Breton called the Surrealists together for a meeting in order to expel Dalí, "who has demonstrated his guilt several times via counter-revolutionary actions designed to glorify the fascism of Hitler".

43. ***The Burning Giraffe***, 1936-1937. Oil on panel. 35 x 27 cm. Kunstmuseum Basel, Basel.

44. ***The Enigma of Hitler***, ca. 1939. Oil on canvas. 51.2 x 79.3 cm. The Reina Sofía National Museum, Madrid.

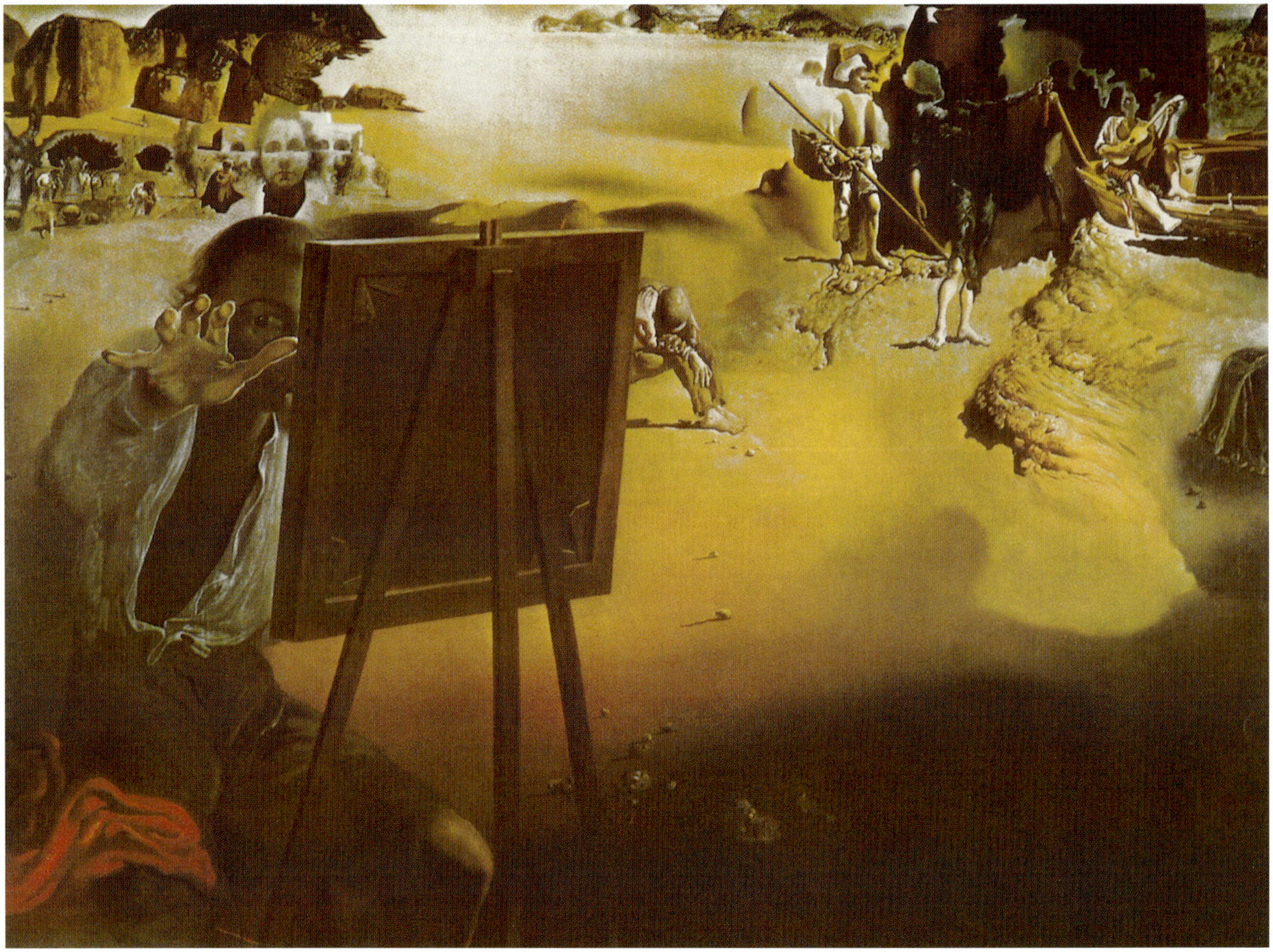

45. ***Impressions of Africa***, 1938.
Oil on canvas.
91.5 x 117.5 cm.
The Boymans-Van Beuningen Museum, Rotterdam.

Dalí appeared at this session on February 5th, 1934, with a thermometer stuck in his mouth, claiming that he had influenza. While he spoke, he kept the thermometer between his lips, and from time to time, read off the temperature. He defended himself against Breton's accusations by stating that the dream of the great language of Surrealism could not be censored by or through logic, morals, or fear. "I closed with the words: 'Therefore, André Breton, if I dream tonight that we make love to one another, tomorrow morning I will paint our most beautiful positions in intercourse with the greatest wealth of detail.' Breton, mortified, his pipe clamped between his teeth, growled: 'I wouldn't like to recommend you do that my friend.' He was checkmated."[26] Dalí ended this grotesque interview by exposing his upper body, kneeling on the floor, and solemnly swearing that he was not an enemy of

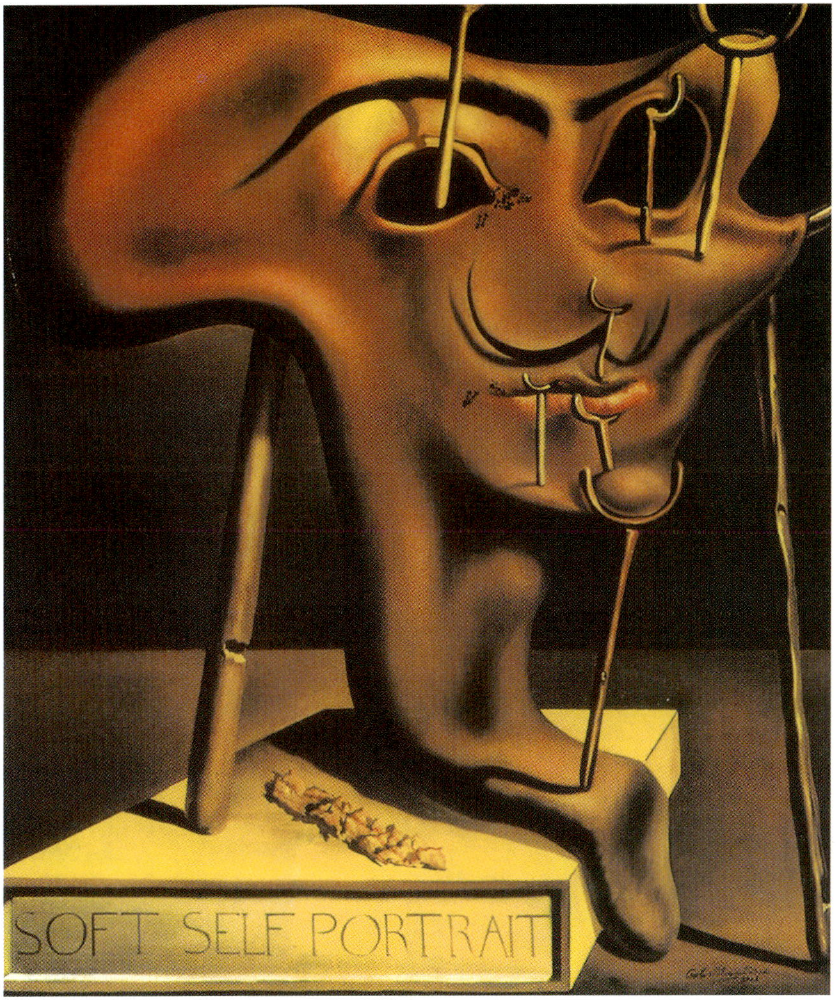

the proletariat. Even after the Paris group had expelled him Dalí still saw himself as a Surrealist, in fact, as the only Surrealist: "The difference between the Surrealists and myself exists in the fact that I am a Surrealist."[27]

The Pictures behind the Pictures. Paranoia as Method

Dalí developed a counterpoint to Breton's artistic procedure of automatism. He did not orient himself towards the dream or towards insanity but found his model in the person who is paranoid because, in contrast to the maniac, this person possesses the "imperialistic power of conviction" to create other visions.

46. ***Soft Self-Portrait with Fried Bacon***, 1941. Oil on canvas. 61.3 x 50.8 cm. The Gala-Salvador Dalí Foundation, Figueras.

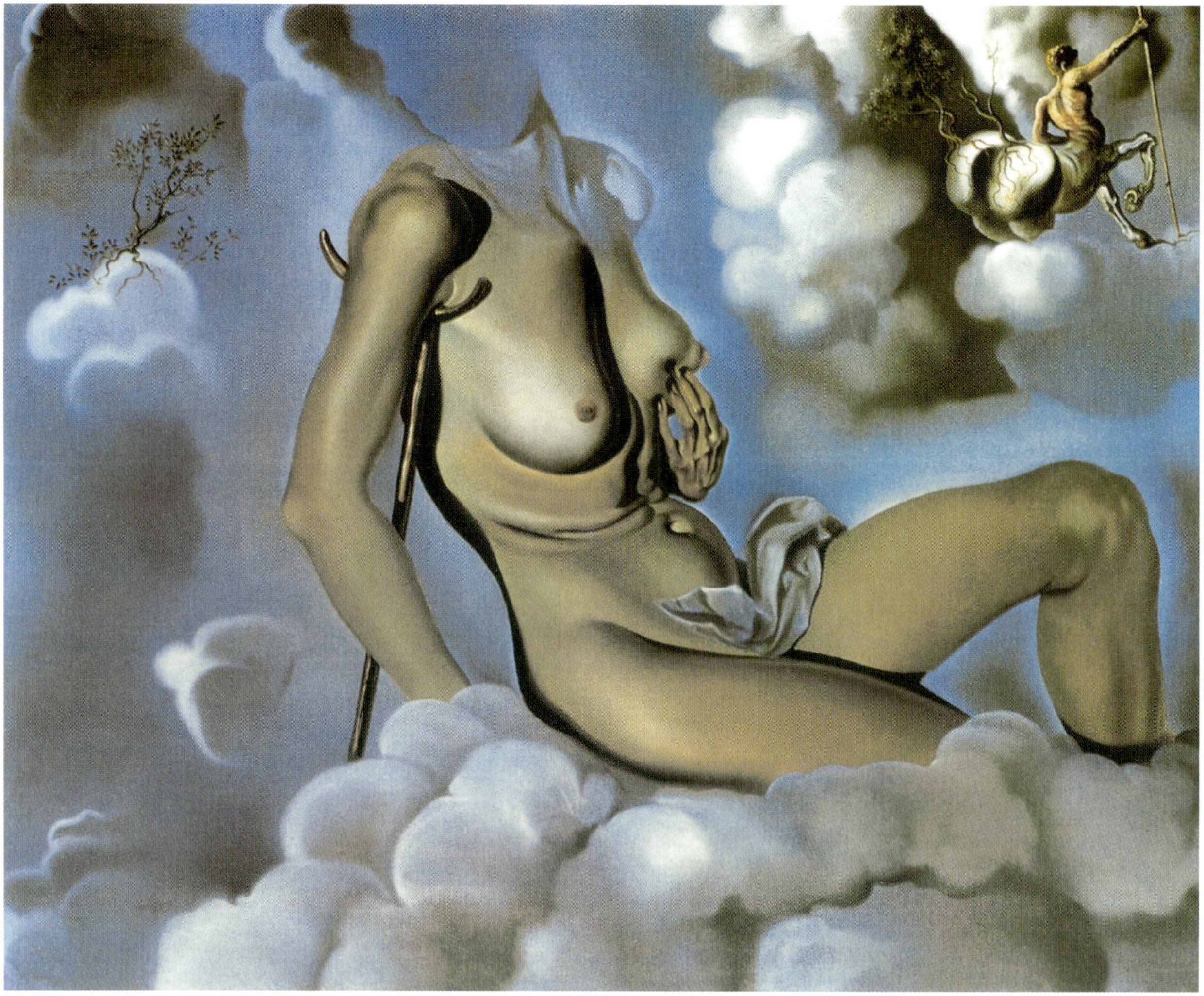

47. ***Honey is Sweeter than Blood***, 1941.
Oil on canvas.
49.5 x 60 cm.
The Santa Barbara Museum of Art.

48. ***Dream Caused by the Flight of a Bee Around a Pomegranate, One Second Before Awakening***, 1944 .
51 x 40.5 cm.
The Thyssen Museum, Madrid.

In addition, the person who suffers from paranoia is capable, by means of his "systematic delusion of interpretation,"[28] of registering subtle differences and emotions. Dalí mentions in his autobiography that even as a child he had already developed the ability to recognize different pictures behind optical appearances. In 1929, Dalí noted various ideas on his concept of the double picture. Gala organized his "confusion of unintelligible scribbles" and published it in 1930 under the title *La femme visible – The Visible Woman*. In the first essay of the collection, titled *The Donkey's Carcass*, Dalí exclaims that paranoiac activity, in contrast to hallucination, is always linked to controllable, continually recognizable materials: "By way of a clear paranoiac process, it becomes possible to receive a double image of perception: that is, the depiction of an object, that without the least physical or anatomical change is simultaneously the depiction of another wholly different object. "[29]

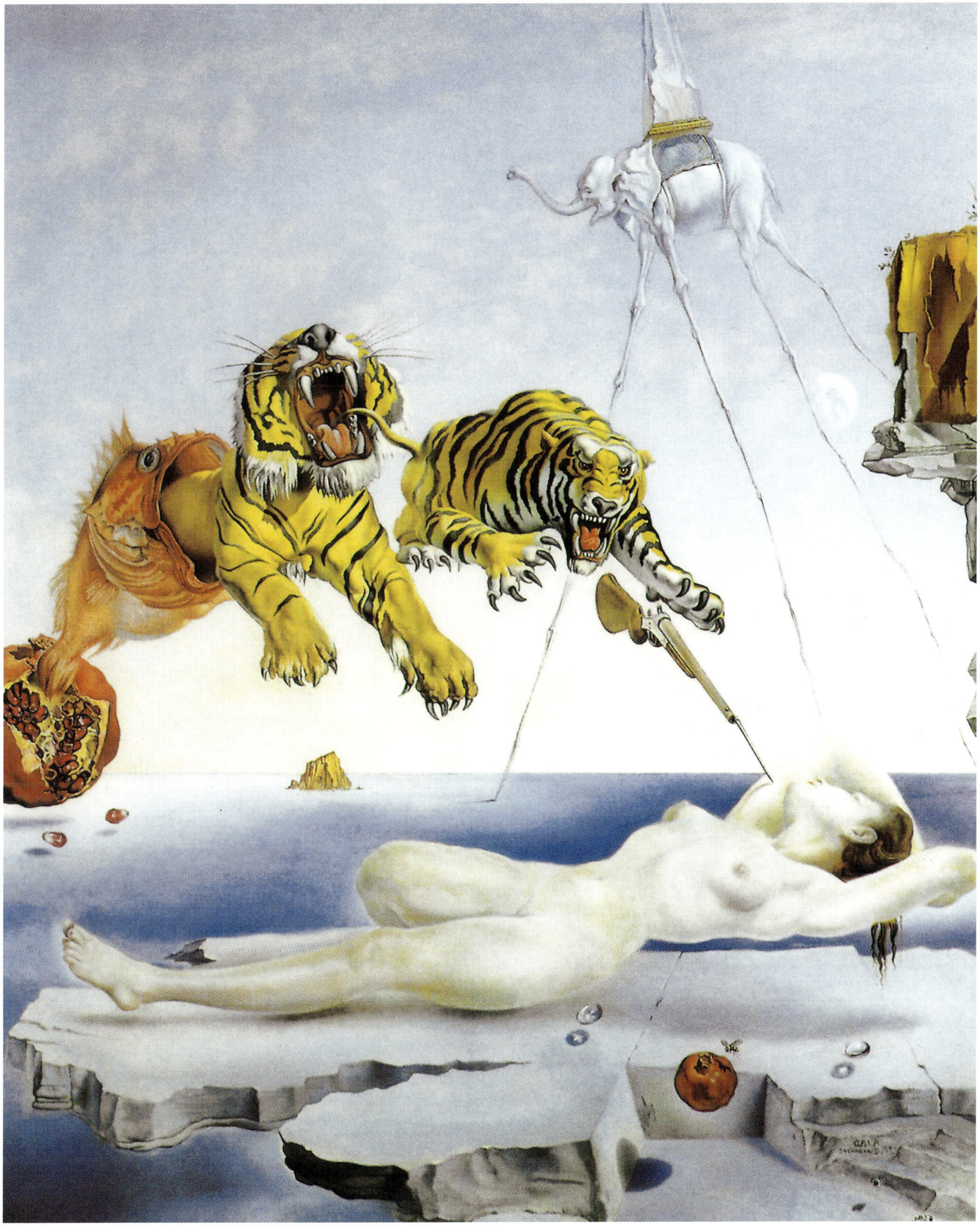

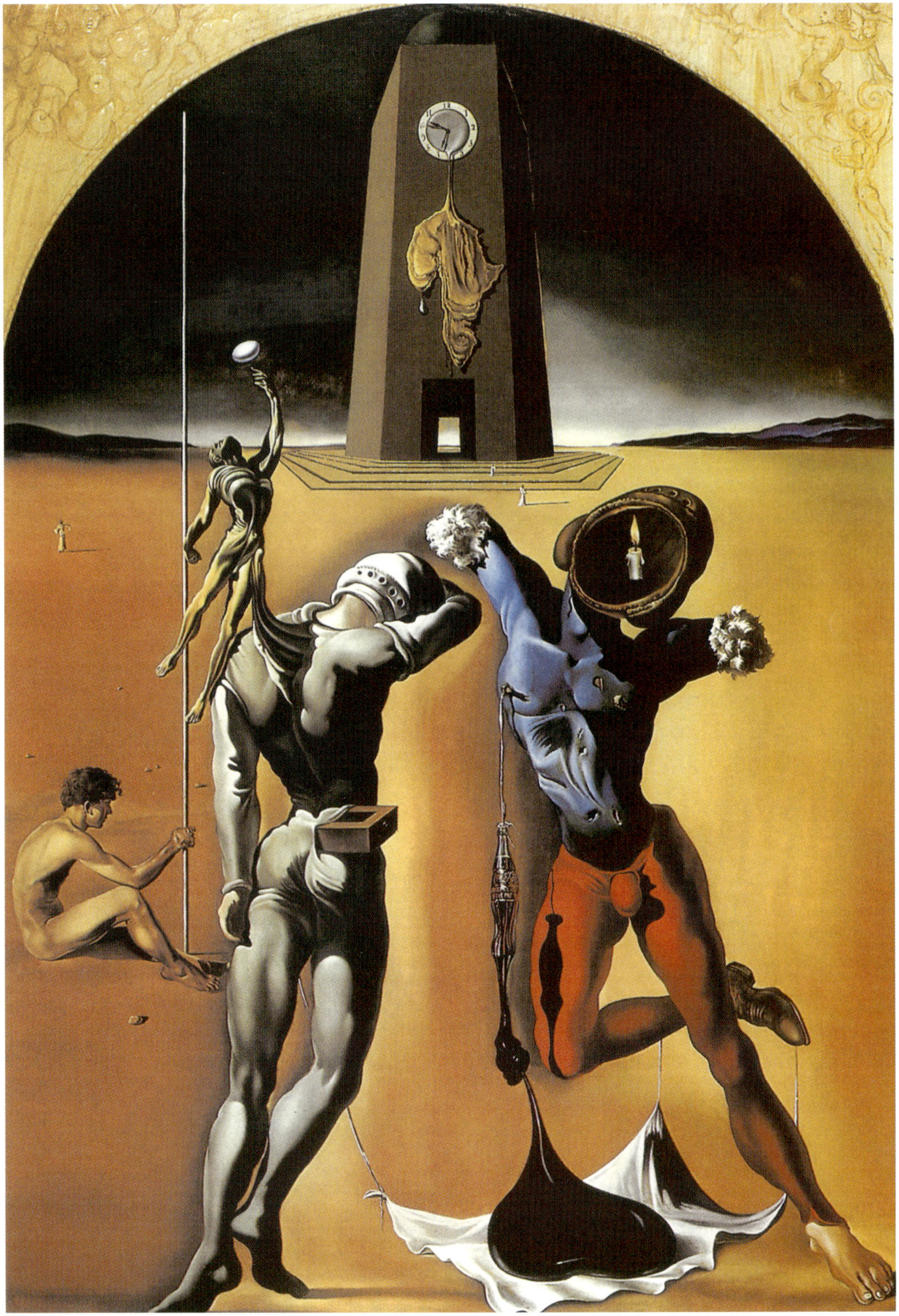

49. ***Poetry of America, the Cosmic Athletes***, 1943. Oil on canvas. 116.8 x 78.7 cm. The Gala-Salvador Dalí Foundation, Figueras.

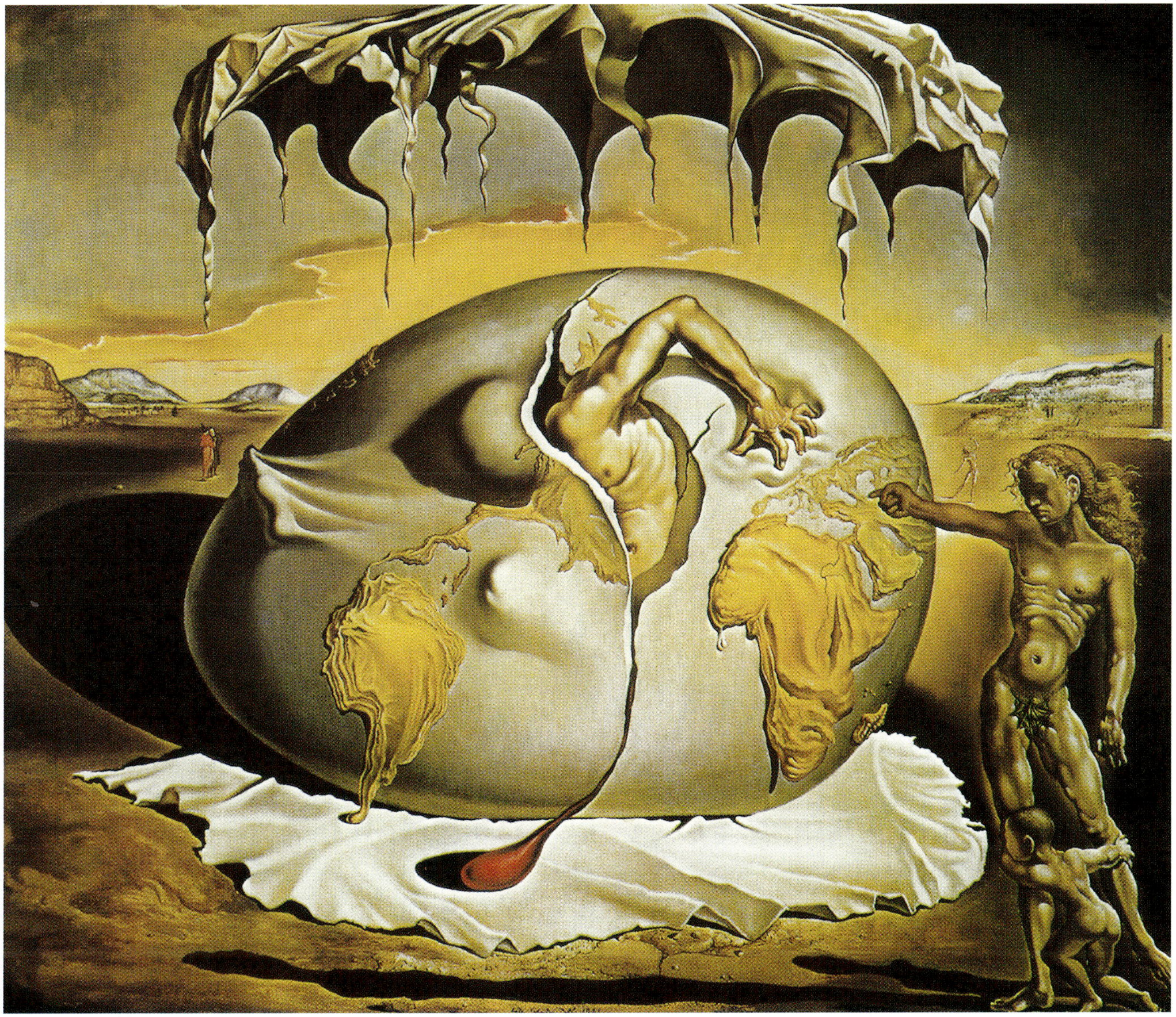

50. ***Geopolitical Child Watching the Birth of the New Man***, 1943. Oil on canvas. 45.5 x 50 cm. The Gala-Salvador Dalí Foundation, Figueras.

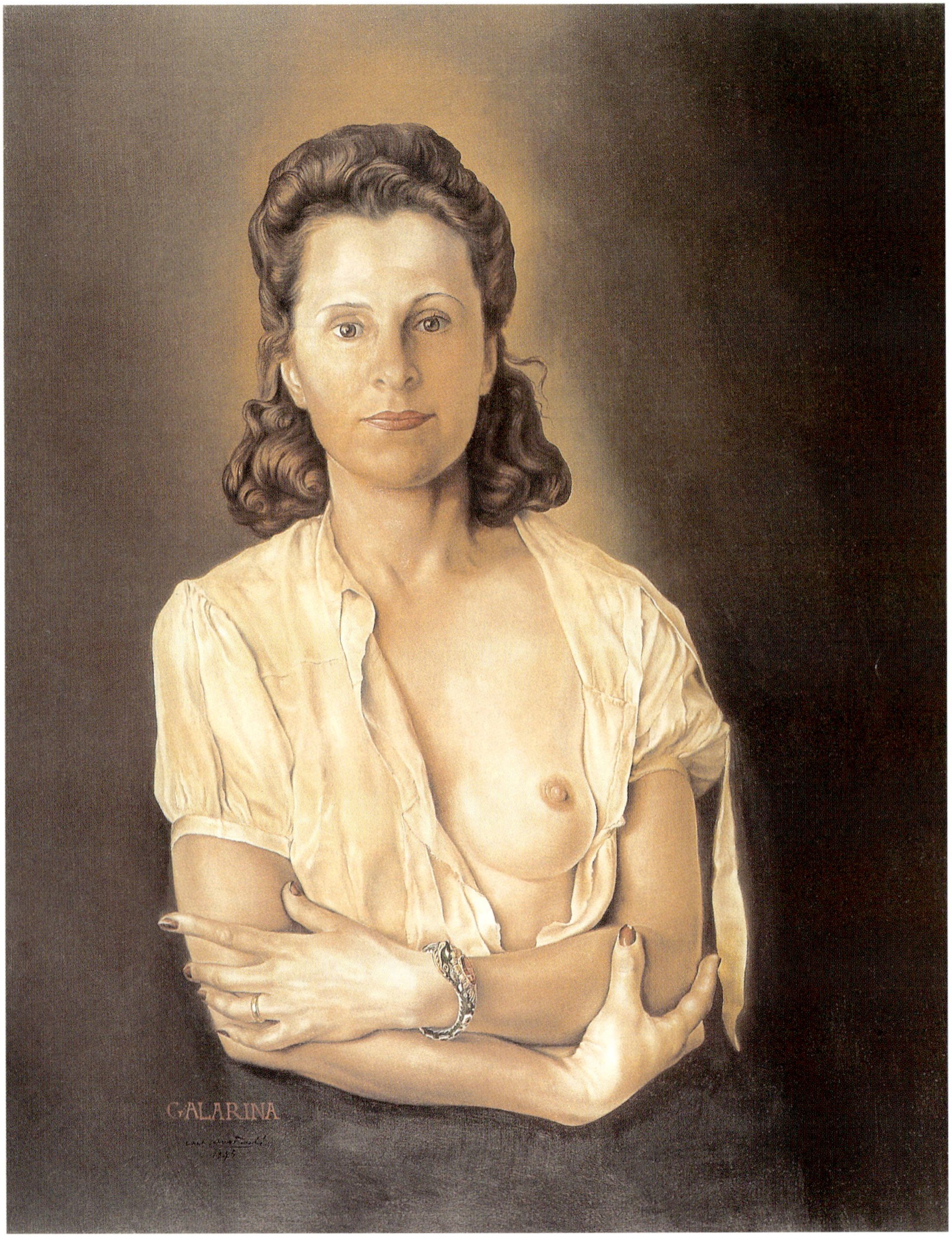

51. ***Galarina***, 1944-1945.
Oil on canvas.
64.1 x 50.2 cm.
The Gala-Salvador
Dalí Foundation,
Figueras.

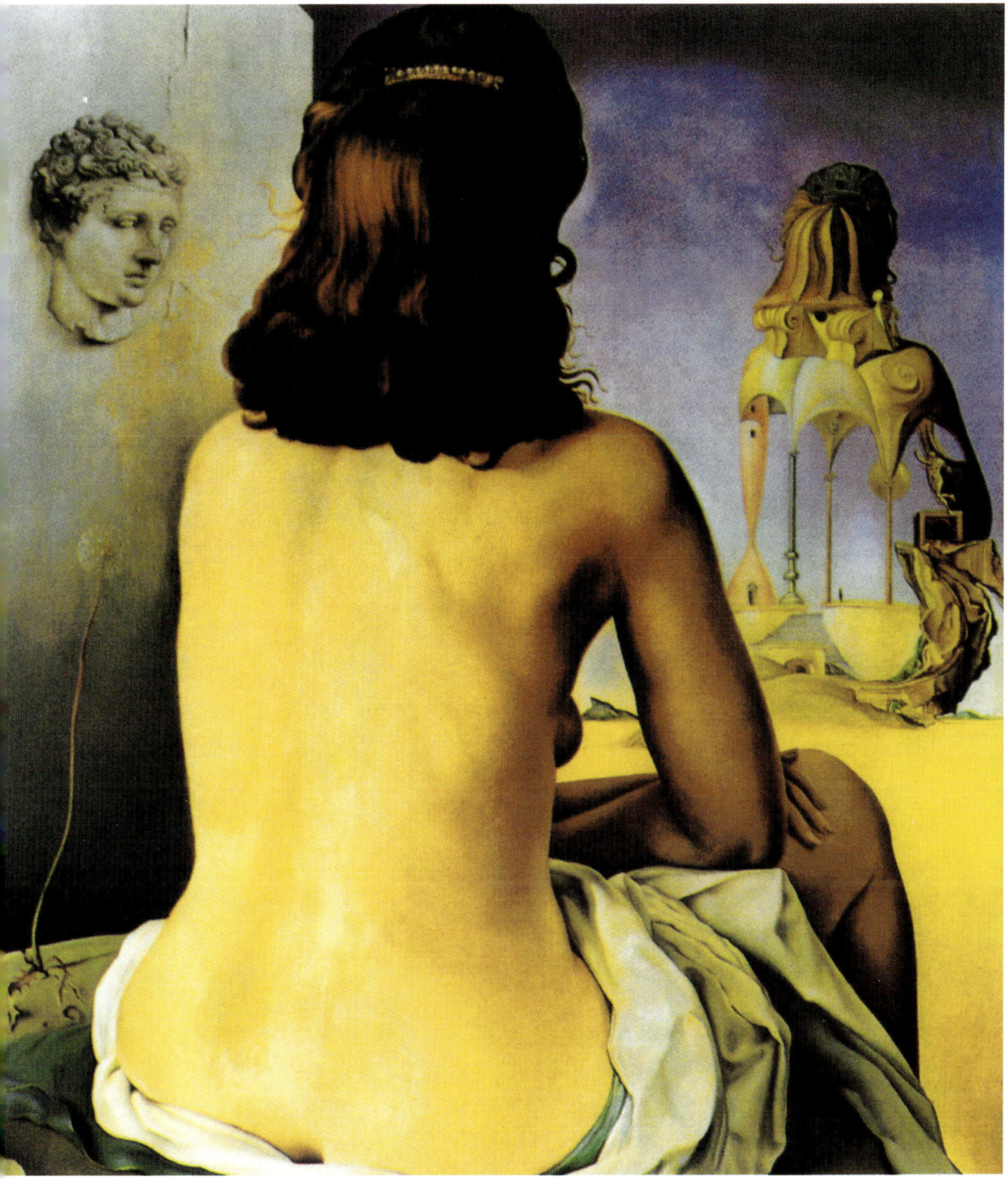

52. ***My Wife, Nude, Contemplating her own Flesh Becoming Stairs, Three Vertebrae of a Column, Sky and Architecture***, 1945.
Oil on panel.
61 x 52 cm.
The José Mugrabi Collection, New York.

Dalí's pictures are the imprint of his "paranoiac clairvoyance". Not seldom does the process of identifying the secret hidden behind superficial appearances continue over many years. Two examples of this are the paintings *Angelus, after Jean-François Millet*, and *The Railway Station at Perpignan*. Dalí had known Millet's painting since his early childhood: "Every time I saw the painting of this farmer and his wife, both standing motionless opposite one another, I experienced an inexplicable sensation of disquiet. The man stands hypnotized – and destroyed – by the mother. He seems to me to take on the attitude of the son rather than the father. One could say that the hat which he holds, and said in the language of Freud, signifies sexual excitement, in order to demonstrate the shameful expression of manhood." At the beginning of the sixties, Dalí learnt that Millet had originally painted a coffin containing their dead son between the farmer and the farmer's wife, later painting over the detail, because it appeared to him to be too melodramatic. Dalí asked the Louvre to make an x-ray of the picture, and it was actually possible to see the outlines of the coffin: "Now everything has been explained! My paranoiac-critical genius had guessed the essentials of the matter."[30] In a similar manner, Dalí found the railway station at Perpignan to be a magical place. Dalí's opinion was that the railway station is an exact model of the universe, the cosmos. He began to measure out the railway station, and organized hundreds of photographs to try and find the hidden secret on the enlarged prints. He found the explanation for his inspiration in 1966, as he learned, "that the measurements of the earth, and of the meter, had been calculated and laid down in Perpignan. A meter is not just the 40 millionth part of the Earth's meridian, it is also the formula for the specific weight of God, and this is the reason why this place appeared to me to be so outstanding. The railway station at Perpignan became transformed into a place of genuine holiness."[31]
Dalí quoted Millet's *Angelus* in many of his paintings. The farming couple also appeared portraying the universe in 1965 in his *Vision of the Farm at Perpignan*.
Independent of other developments, the paranoic-critical method remained the basic principle in Dalí's work. The analysis however, did not always take place over a series of years. Often discoveries in the form of spontaneous over-blending occured, as in the case of his renowned melting watches. Dalí discusses the genesis of the painting, *The Persistence of Memory* in his autobiography: "Having concluded our dinner with a very strong Camembert and after the others had gone, I remained sitting quietly at the table for a long time considering the philosophical problem of 'Super-Softs' that the cheese had brought to my attention. I stood up, went into my atelier and turned on the light to take one last look at the picture I was presently working on, as was my habit.

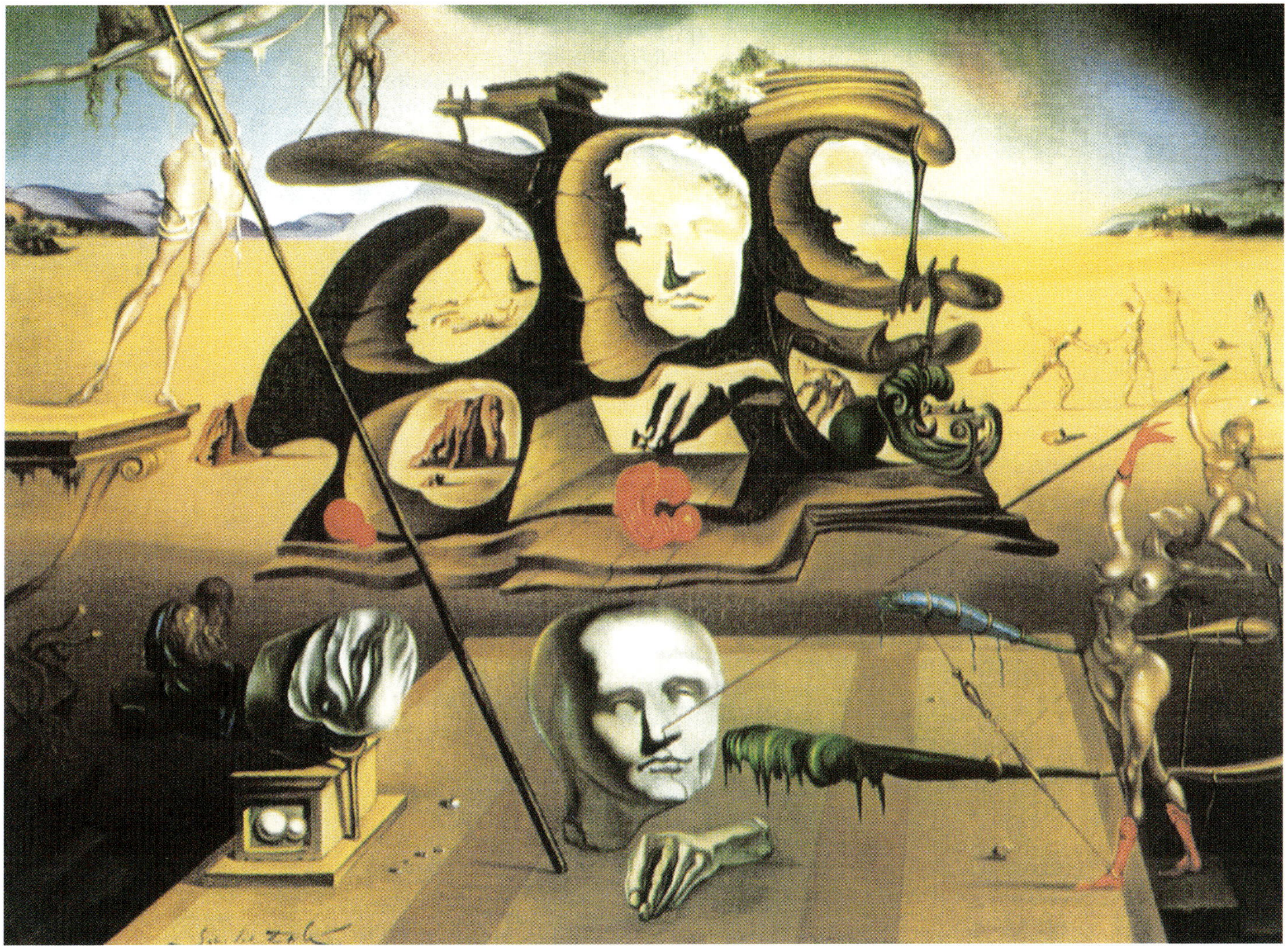

This picture depicts the landscape at Port Lligat; the cliffs lie in a transparent, melancholy dusk light and an olive-tree with severed branches devoid of leaves stands in the foreground. I knew that the atmosphere which I had been able to create with this landscape was the background for an idea that would serve to create a surprising picture but I didn't know in the slightest what it would be. I was just about to turn off the light when I suddenly 'saw' the answer. I saw two melting watches, one hanging pathetically over the branch of the olive-tree. Although my headache had become so strong that I was suffering, I readied my palette impatiently and got down to work."[32]

53. ***Napoleon's Nose, Transformed into a Pregnant Woman, Walking his Shadow with Melancholia Amongst Original Ruins***, 1945.
Oil on canvas.
51 x 65.5 cm.
The G.E.D Nahmad Collection, Geneva.

Between Worlds. First Successes in America

In November of 1934, Dalí and Gala travelled to the United States for the first time. Dalí's work had been known there since the end of the twenties. Julien Levy, who was one of the first to introduce the European Surrealists to the USA, exhibited Dalí's pictures in several group exhibitions, and in the winter of 1933, he devoted his first single exhibition to him. Dalí's exhibition at the Levy gallery in 1934 was criticised by some newspapers as being a "fashion show" but for the public it was an unrivalled success. The New World offered Dalí unbridled possibilities for celebrating the sensational and eccentric. Shortly before the Dalí's returned to the Old World in January 1935, Caresse Crosby organized a parting celebration at the elegant New York restaurant Coq Rouge. This "dream-ball" has gone down in history as the first Surrealist's ball. Dalí was impressed by the crazy ideas of the guests: "Society women appeared with their heads stuck in bird-cages and otherwise practically naked. [...]In the middle of the staircase a bathtub full of water had been hung, which threatened to fall down and empty its contents over the heads of the guests at any moment. And in the corner of the hall hung a butcher's hook with a whole, hollowed-out ox hanging from it, the gaping belly of which was held open with crutches, and stuffed full with half a dozen gramophones."[33] On their arrival in Paris, the atmosphere in the French capital felt oppressive for Dalí: the Surrealists were getting caught up in political conflict. He decided to escape with Gala to the isolation of Port Lligat. The peace on the Catalan coast did not last for long. In Barcelona, the first bombs were exploding – an antecedent to the Civil War. The Dalí's decided to travel. Until 1940, they remained constantly en route. Twice in the winter of 1936/1937 and in January 1939 they traveled to the USA. In between times they lived in Italy and the south of France. Dalí decided "decisively" that he was not a historical person. The war also failed to alter his point of view. In pictures like *Soft Construction with Boiled Beans – Premonition of the Civil War*, he showed his vision of the carnage. The political dimension of the state of affairs in his fatherland, however, did not interest him at all. He instead turned to studying the painting of the Renaissance. In Dalí's opinion, the history of the time was not reflected in the conversations of the Surrealists in the cafés of Montmarte, but at the Place Vendôme, in the heart of the fashion world. Dalí had befriended the fashion-designers Coco Chanel and Elsa Schiaparelli. Dalí drafted a perfume bottle in the form of a golden mussel for the latter as well as a shoe-hat and some clothing. These excursions into the world of design brought him into bad favour in the art world.

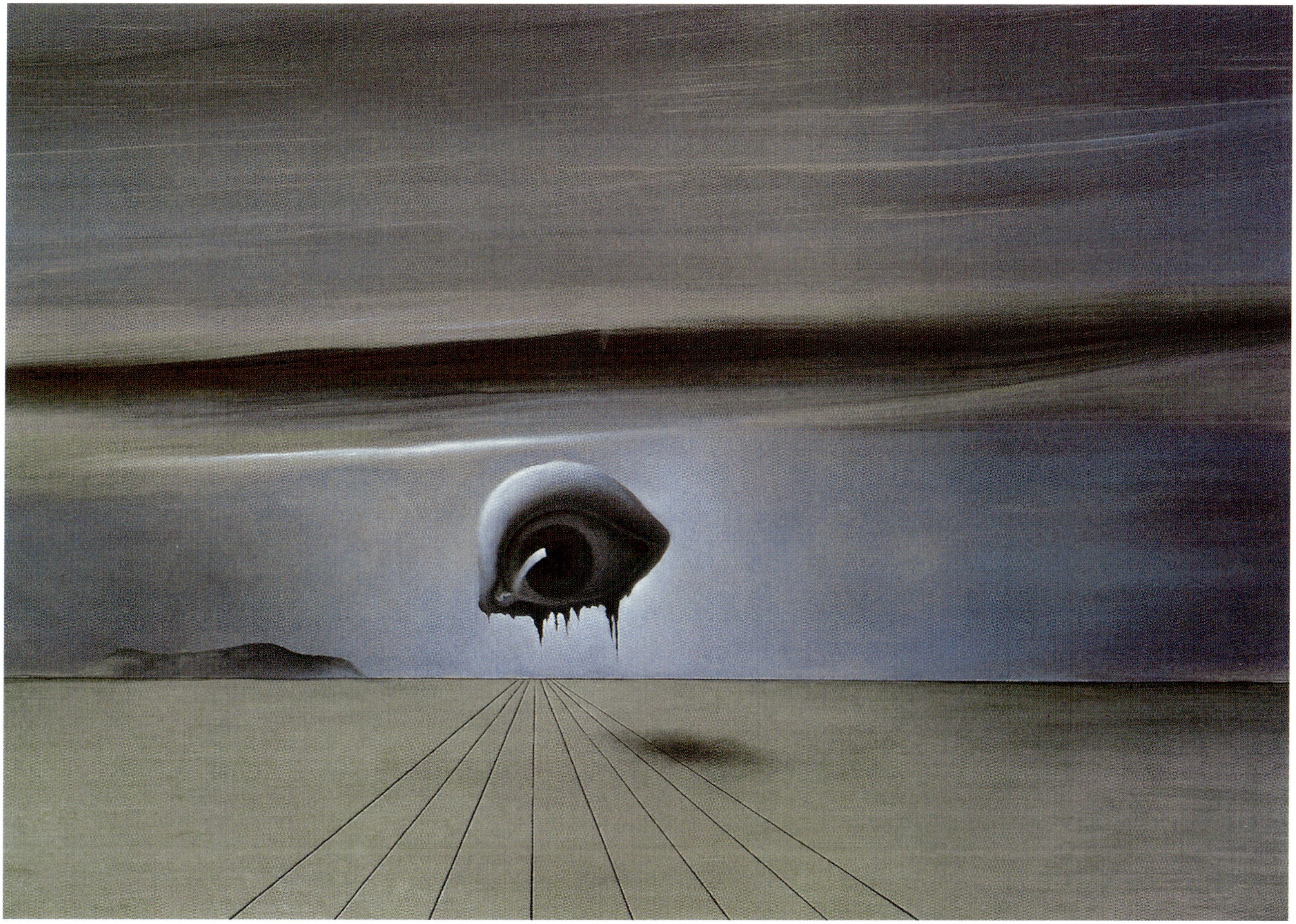

André Breton formed the anagram "Avida Dollars" – "dollar hungry" – out of the letters of the name Salvador Dalí. Dalí was in the process of achieving his goal: becoming famous not just amongst a small circle of discerning artist-friends but to a much larger audience as well. On his second trip to New York in December 1936, *Time* magazine devoted the title page to him. It featured a portrait that Man Ray had taken of him. The day after the opening of his second single exhibition at the Levy gallery, all twenty-five paintings and twelve drawings were sold.

54. ***The Eye – Design for "Spellbound"***, 1945.
Oil on panel.
Dimensions unknown
Private collection.

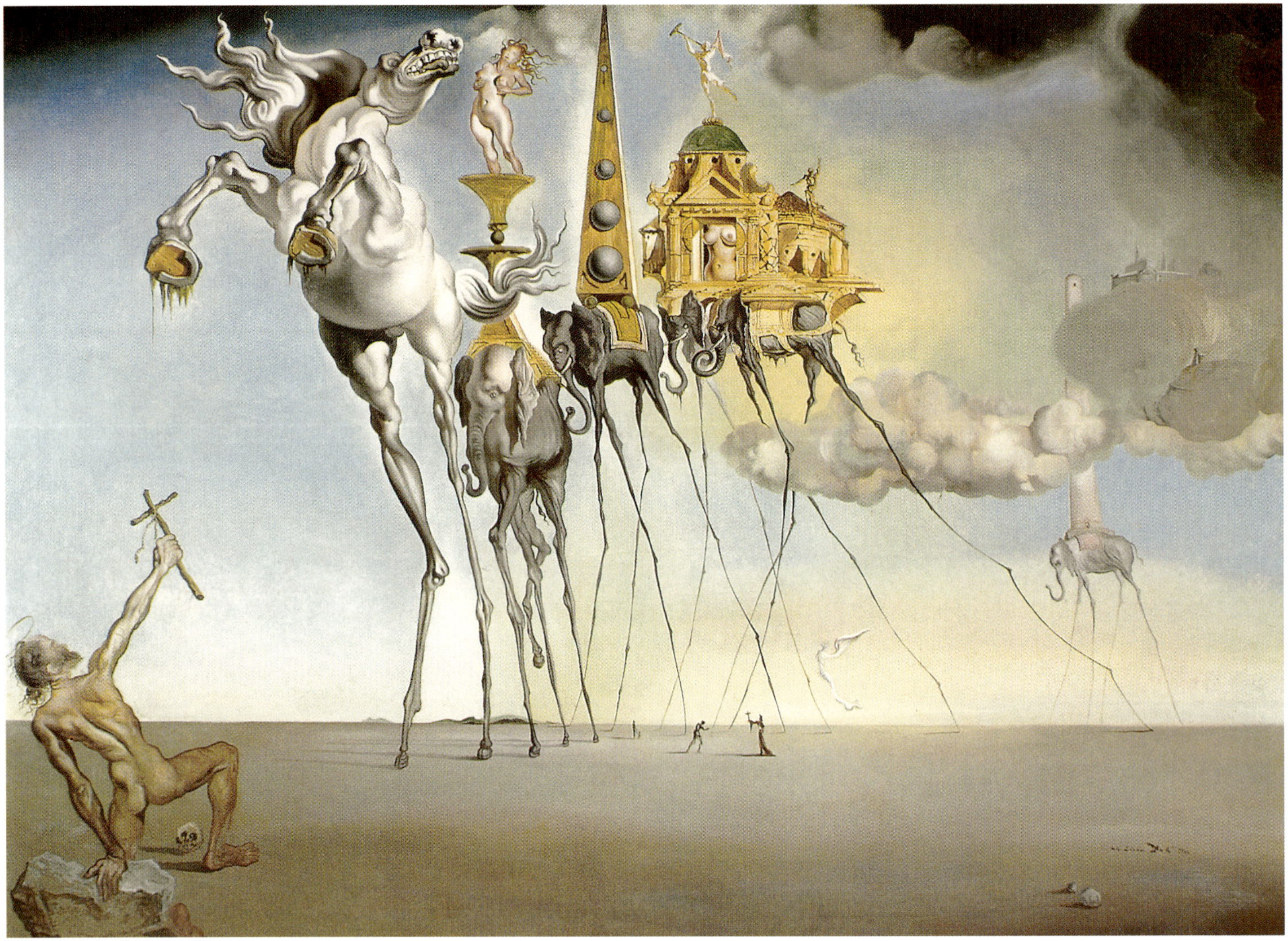

55. ***The Temptation of Saint Anthony***, 1946.
Oil on canvas.
89.7 x 119.5 cm
The Royal Museums of Fine Arts of Belgium, Brussels.

56. ***Leda Atomica***, 1949.
Oil on canvas.
61.1 x 45.6 cm.
The Gala-Salvador Dalí Foundation, Figueras.

Dalí was showered with offers of work. For the New York luxury department store Bonwit-Teller on Fifth Avenue, he decorated a display window: "I used a jointed-doll, with a head made out of red roses and fingernails of ermine. On a table stood a telephone that turned into a lobster; and over the chair hung my famous, aphrodisiac jacket."[34] Dalí started a fashionable trend with this decoration: when he returned to New York two years later, he noticed that an array of display windows on the elegant shopping-street had been decorated à la Dalí. In order to demonstrate the difference between the real and the imitated Surrealist decorations, he designed two further displays for Bonwit-Teller. This time, he used dusty old wax-dolls from the year 1900, which he had found in the attic at the department store.

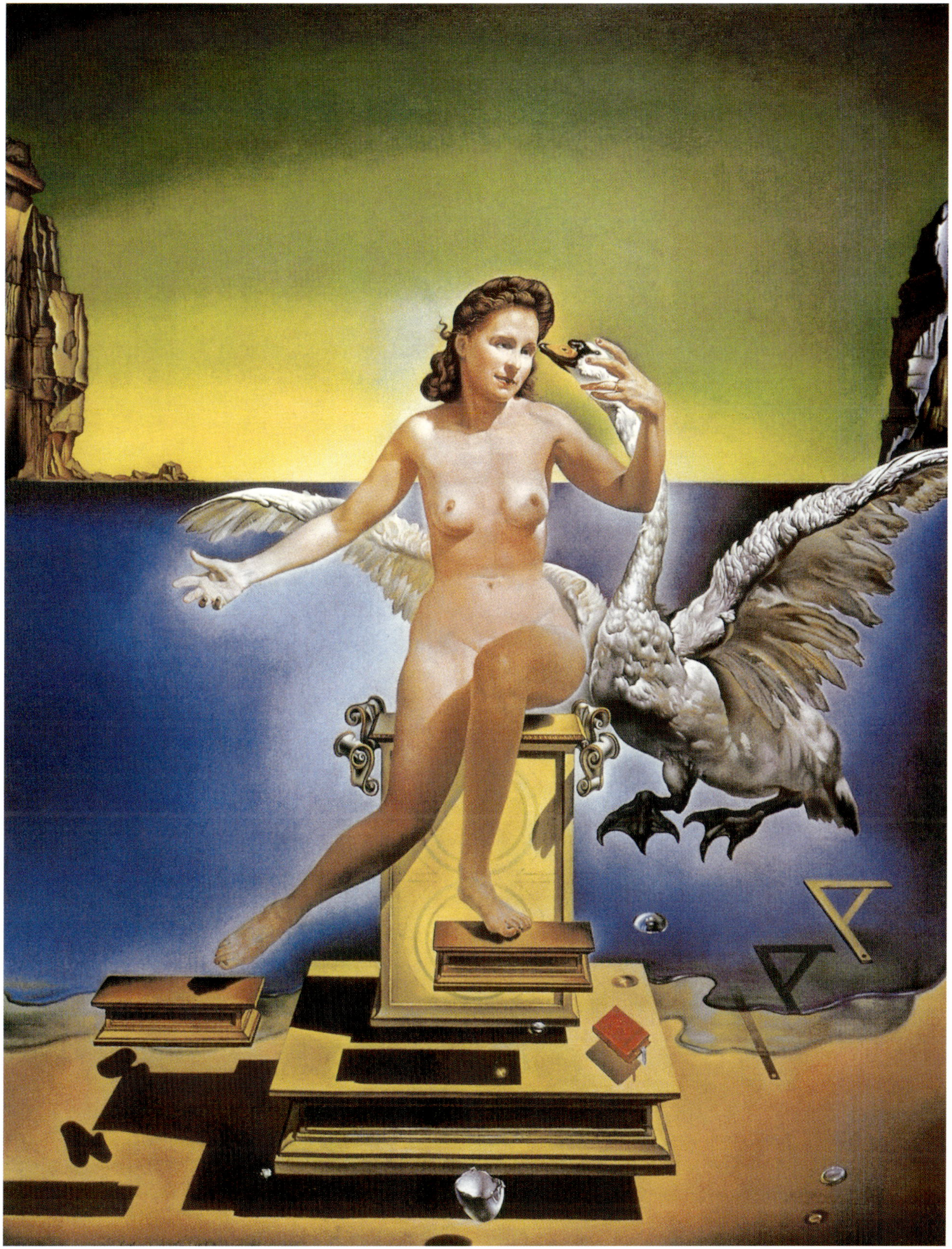

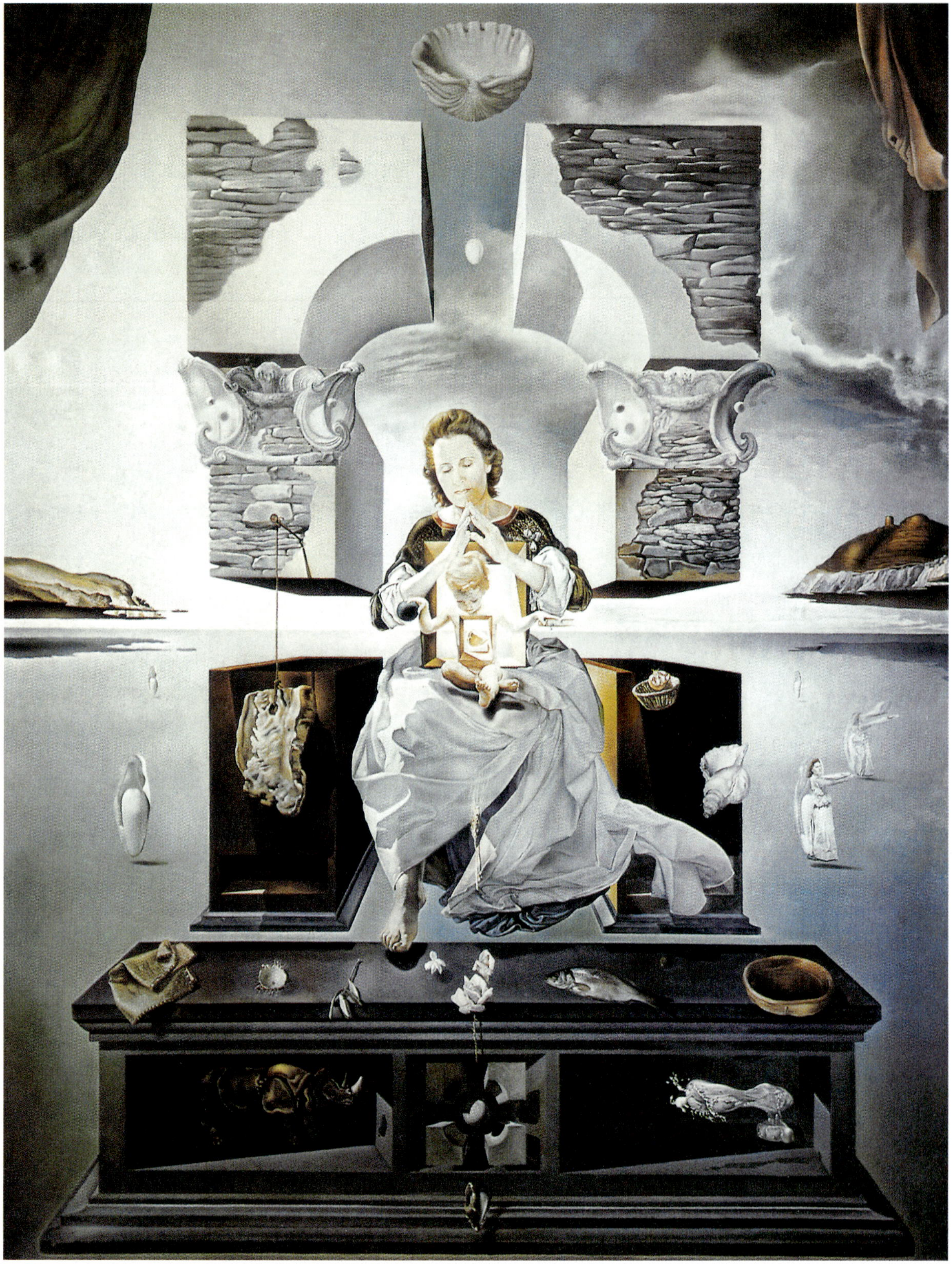

57. ***The Madonna of Port Lligat***, 1950. Oil on canvas. 144 x 96 cm. Private collection, Tokyo.

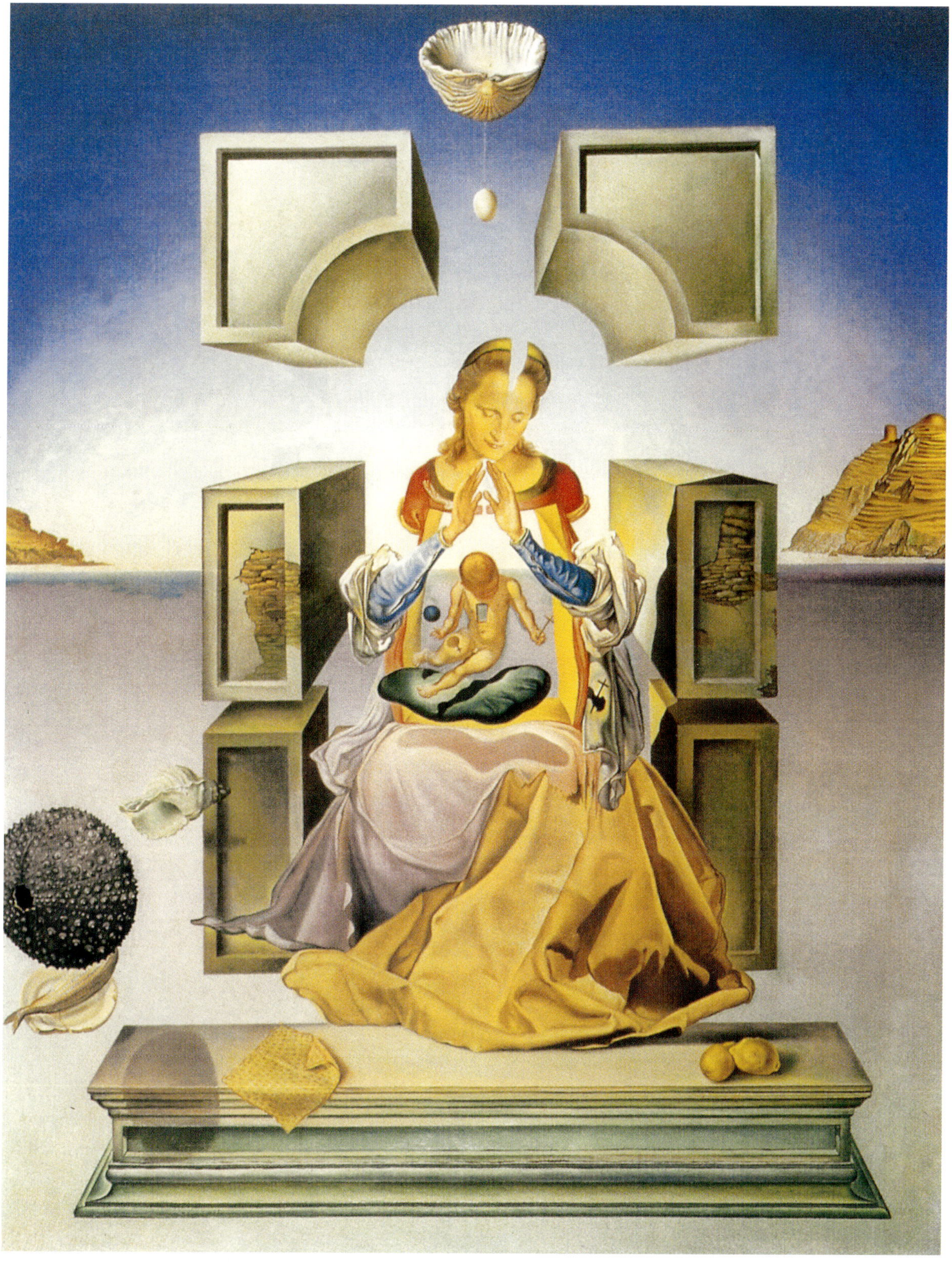

58. ***The Madonna of Port Lligat***, 1949.
Oil on canvas,
48.9 x 37.5 cm.
Marquette University,
Haggerty Museum of
Art, Milwaukee.

As Bonwit-Teller changed this decoration a day later – the dolls were exchanged for others, the burning bed was removed – Dalí smashed-in the display window. He spent a night in prison. In the press, he was lauded for his open fight for the "independence of American art, which all too often is threatened by the inefficiency of industrial and commercially oriented middlemen."[35] In Europe war had begun. In their search for a place to live, the Dalí's combined the possibility of Nazi invasion "with gastronomical potential". They chose Arcachon near Bordeaux and moved into a large villa built in the colonial-style. In June, however, the first bombs began to fall on Bordeaux. The Dalí's decided to escape to the USA. Dalí took a detour via Figueras. He visited his father and sister, whom he had not seen for eleven years.
The Civil War had also left scars on his family home – his sister had been tortured by the military intelligence and been driven into madness. A bomb had destroyed the balcony on the house. The tiled floor in the dining room had been blackened by fire. Nevertheless, Dalí found that in itself, "fundamentally", nothing had changed. The visit to Figueras supported Dalí's belief that the war in Europe would not bring any change. In his opinion, the old world destroyed itself, not to give birth to something new, but instead to return to the roots of tradition. Dalí already sensed the coming renaissance and began to work on a cosmogony, on a world design, created by Dalí, the divine. He accepted his departure to the USA by reasoning that he needed a quiet place to prepare the genesis of his world design. Arriving in the USA, Dalí wrote his autobiography. It was an act of shedding his skin – he stripped off his hitherto existing life.

Break out into Tradition

The Renaissance of the Universal Genius as Marketing Expert

Dalí saw himself as a universal genius in the sense of Leonardo da Vinci. He had always worked in a variety of different disciplines besides painting: he had studied philosophy and psychoanalysis, had written scripts, had designed furniture and clothing, had created scenery and costumes for drama and opera and had choreographed a ballet. The break which Dalí decided upon at the beginning of his eight-year stay in the New World was primarly based on the decision to transform the name that he had acquired into a lucrative market. The moustache became his trademark. A decisive role here was played by the photographer Philippe Halsman. One of the first photographs by Halsman taken of the artist at the beginning of the nineteen-forties, shows Dalí in tails, in front of a skull formed out of naked women's bodies, sporting a top hat and cane.

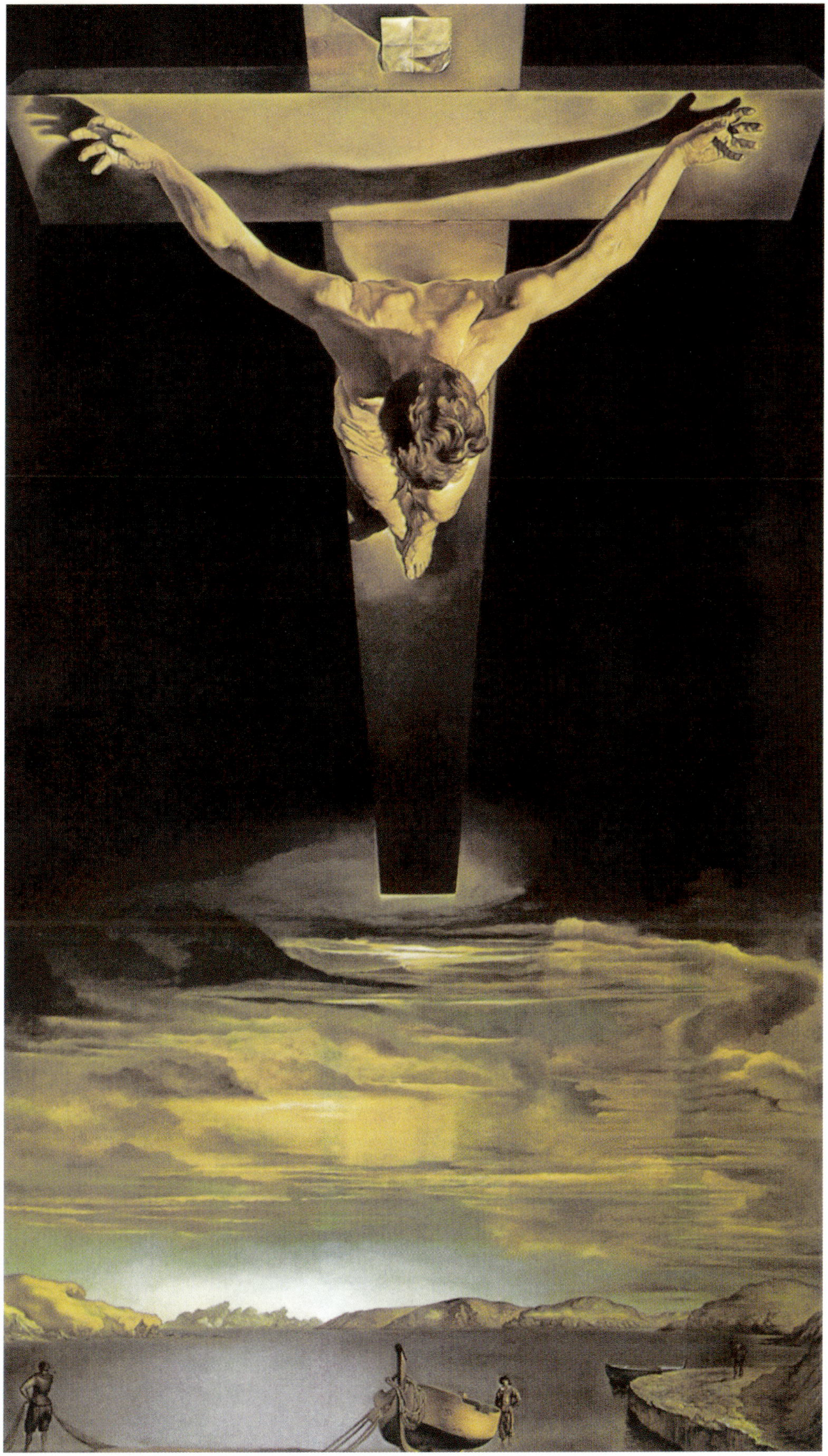

59. ***Christ of Saint John of the Cross***, 1951.
Oil on canvas.
205 x 166.
The Glasgow Art Gallery, Glasgow.

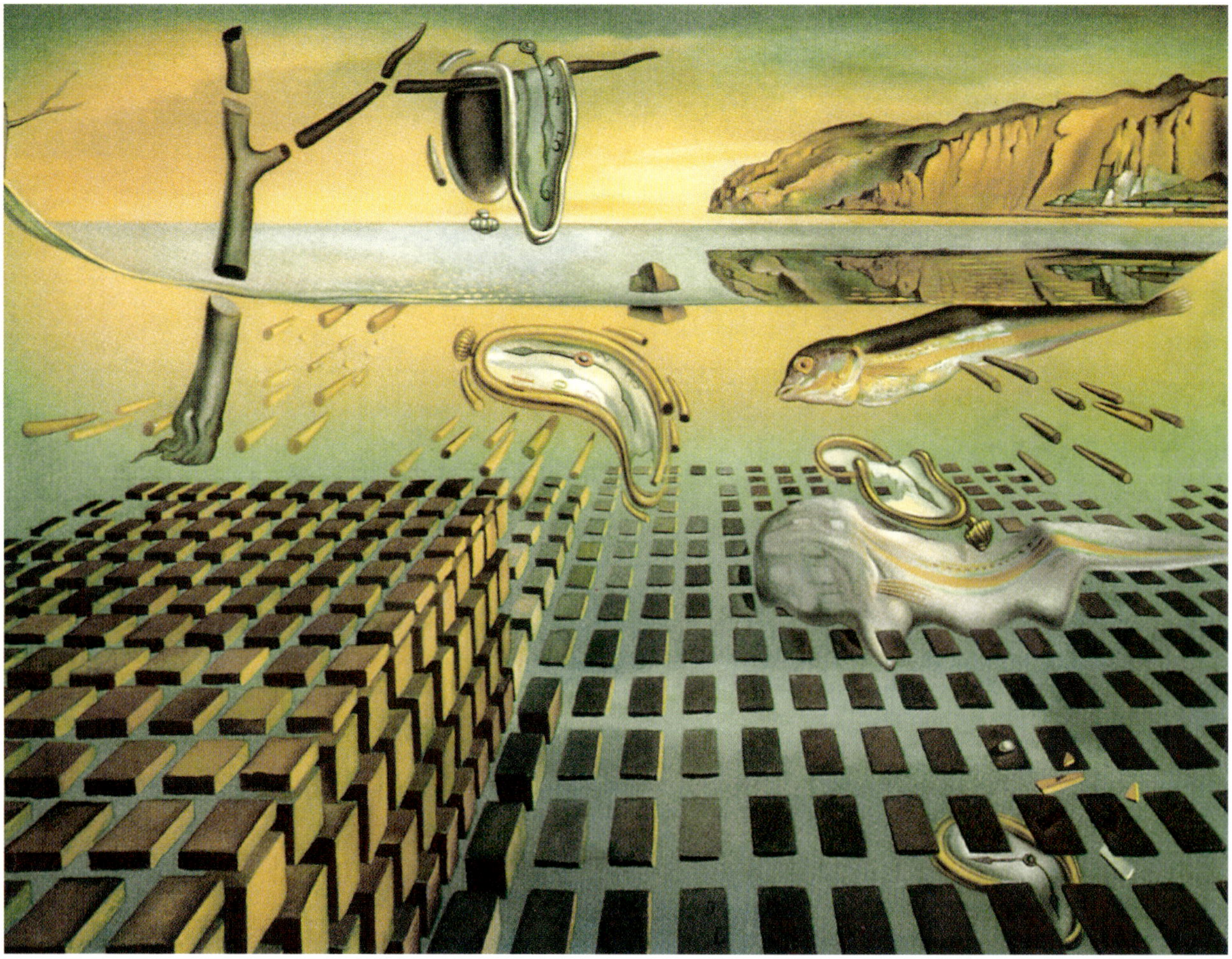

60. ***Desintegration of the Persistance of Memory***, 1952-1954. Oil on canvas. 25 x 33 cm. The Salvador Dalí Museum, St Petersburg (FL).

Dalí stylized himself as an art object. In depicting himself, the painter was continually and thoroughly ironic: for one of the photos he transforms his moustache into a dollar-sign – an allusion to Breton's anagram "Avida Dollars". Dalí never denied his desire for wealth. He could never get enough of fame or money, as he stated in an interview in 1975.[36] And in the forties, both of these achieved untold proportions.

At the end of 1942, the New York Museum of Modern Art put on a retrospective of Dalí's work featuring fifty pictures and seventeen drawings. In December 1942 Dalí met Eleanor and Reynolds Morse. Four months later the Morses bought their first "Dalí" for 1,200 dollars. In the following years the price for his works increased continually. However, the most important source of income for Dalí was not his picture sales, even though some single paintings did sell at up to 300,000 dollars. He earned much more from client contracts: he designed ties and ashtrays, created advertisements for perfumes

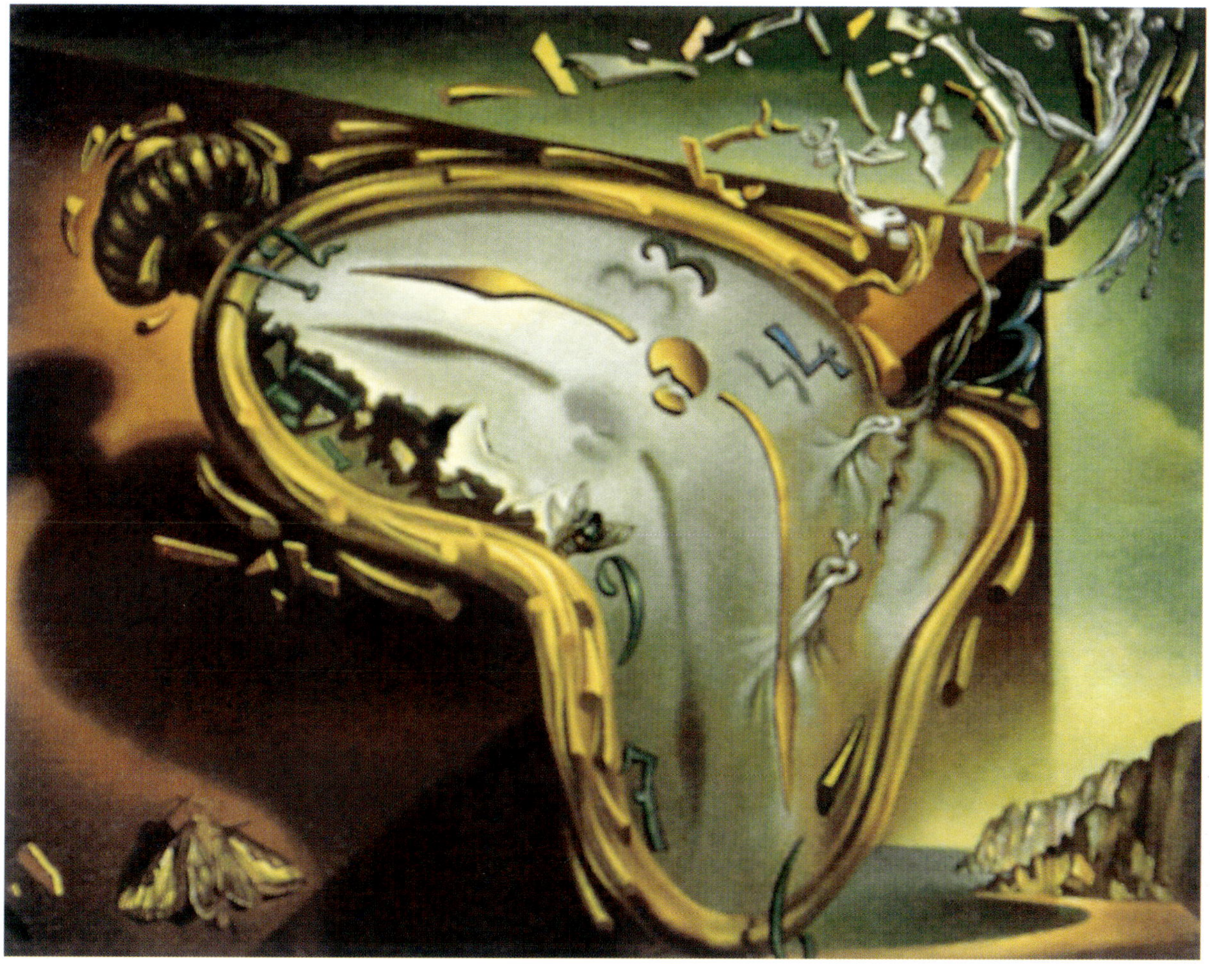

and nylon stockings, designed the title page of the magazines *Vogue* and *Esquire*. In the house of the millionaire Helena Rubenstein he painted three large frescoes. He illustrated numerous books, amongst them Cervantes' *Don Quixote* and Shakespeare's *Macbeth*. Besides this, Dalí carried on his work in the theater. After the performance of his frequently reworked drama *Bacchantal* in 1939, he wrote the libretto for a ballet with motifs from the Ariadne myth. Under the leadership of Leonide Massine, *Labyrinth* was premiered by the Ballets russes at the Metropolitan Opera on October 8th, 1941. The scenery consisted of a gigantic bust of a naked man with a lowered head. On the breast of the man gaped the entrance to the labyrinth. The proximity to Hollywood enticed Dalí back to film again. As early as his second visit to the USA in 1936, Dalí had visited the dream factory. In 1945, the director Alfred Hitchcock brought Dalí into the studio to create the dream-sequence for his psychoanalytically inspired film *Spellbound*.

61. ***Explosion***, 1954.
Oil on canvas.
20.5 x 25.7 cm
Private collection.

Hitchcock had envisaged dream sequences of particular visual sharpness for his film: "Up until this point, the dream-pictures in films had always consisted of a halo surrounded by a whirlpool of purposefully effervescent clouds with people moving back and forth in a mixture of stage-snow and mist. This was the unquestioned norm and I was determined to do the opposite. I chose Dalí [...] because of his ability to paint with hallucinogenic accuracy, which expressed the exact opposite of these evaporations and steamings."[37] Not all of Dalí's ideas were used during the filming, however. For example, the studio refused to hang fifteen pianos from the ceiling. And so Dalí refrained from using the corresponding sequence and created a new setting. Among other things, the dream-sequence is set in a nightclub, where the curtains are painted with large eyes being cut by a man holding a large pair of scissors – suggestive of the entrance-scene in *Un Chien andalou*. As a medium, Dalí considered film to be a "secondary form". However, he did become more and more attracted to its technical possibilities. A few months after his successful work with Hitchcock, Walt Disney courted the artist: Dalí was supposed to create a six-minute sequence for an animation film with the title *Fantasia*. Together with the graphic artist John Hench he developed the screenplay. But then Disney dropped him from the project. In 1950, Dalí worked on another film. He created the dream-sequence for Vincente Minelli's comedy *The Bride's Father*. As a result of these many activities, the painter faded more and more into the background. Dalí's turning to classicism carried itself over onto the screen only marginally. Since his arrival in the USA, Dalí did not come any further with his world design, which proved to be a difficult birth. However, the dropping of the first atomic bomb over Hiroshima gave way to the first contractions: "The explosion of the atomic bomb on August 6th, 1945, jarred me seismically. From this point onwards, the atom became the first object of my considerations. Many landscapes that I painted at this time express the enormous fear I felt on being notified of this explosion."[38] Religion and science became new topics for Dalían painting. In 1946, he painted his first piece of work with a religious motif: *The Temptation of Saint Anthony*. In Dalí's version, Saint Anthony is threatened by a rearing horse and spindle-legged elephants. In 1948, Dalí converted to the Roman Catholic Church. In the same year he returned once more to Europe.

62. ***The Maximum Speed of Raphaël's Madonna***, 1954. Oil on canvas. 81.2 x 66 cm. The Reina Sofía National Museum, Madrid.

Metamorphosis to Divine. The Time of Honour and Riches

"Bienvenida a Salvador Dalí": *Destino* magazine greeted the famous son with this cry as he returned to his fatherland. In 1948, Dalí and Gala moved back into their house in Port Lligat. There, in the place that had retained such special meaning for him since his childhood days, Dalí underwent his metamorphosis to sainthood, to the divine:

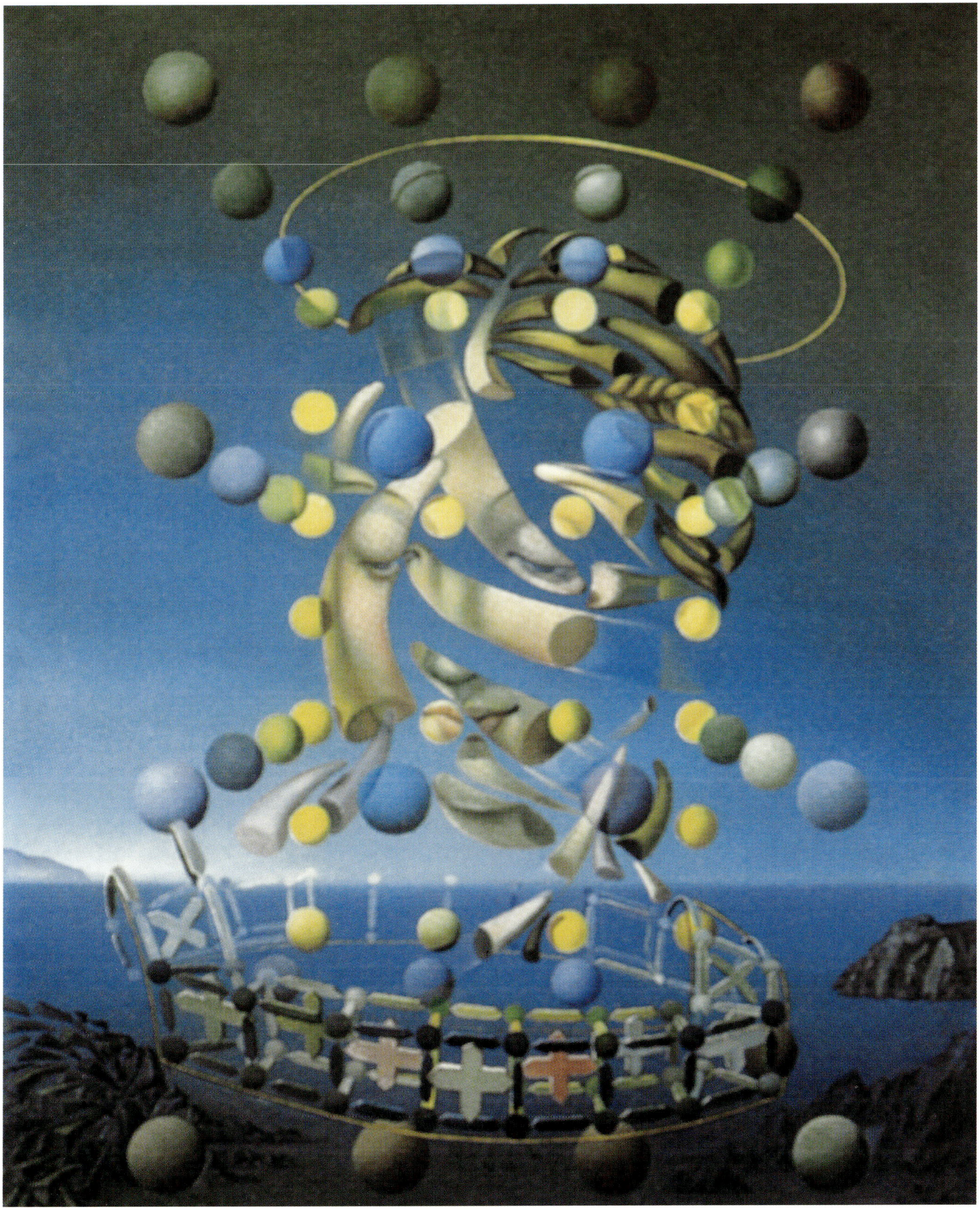

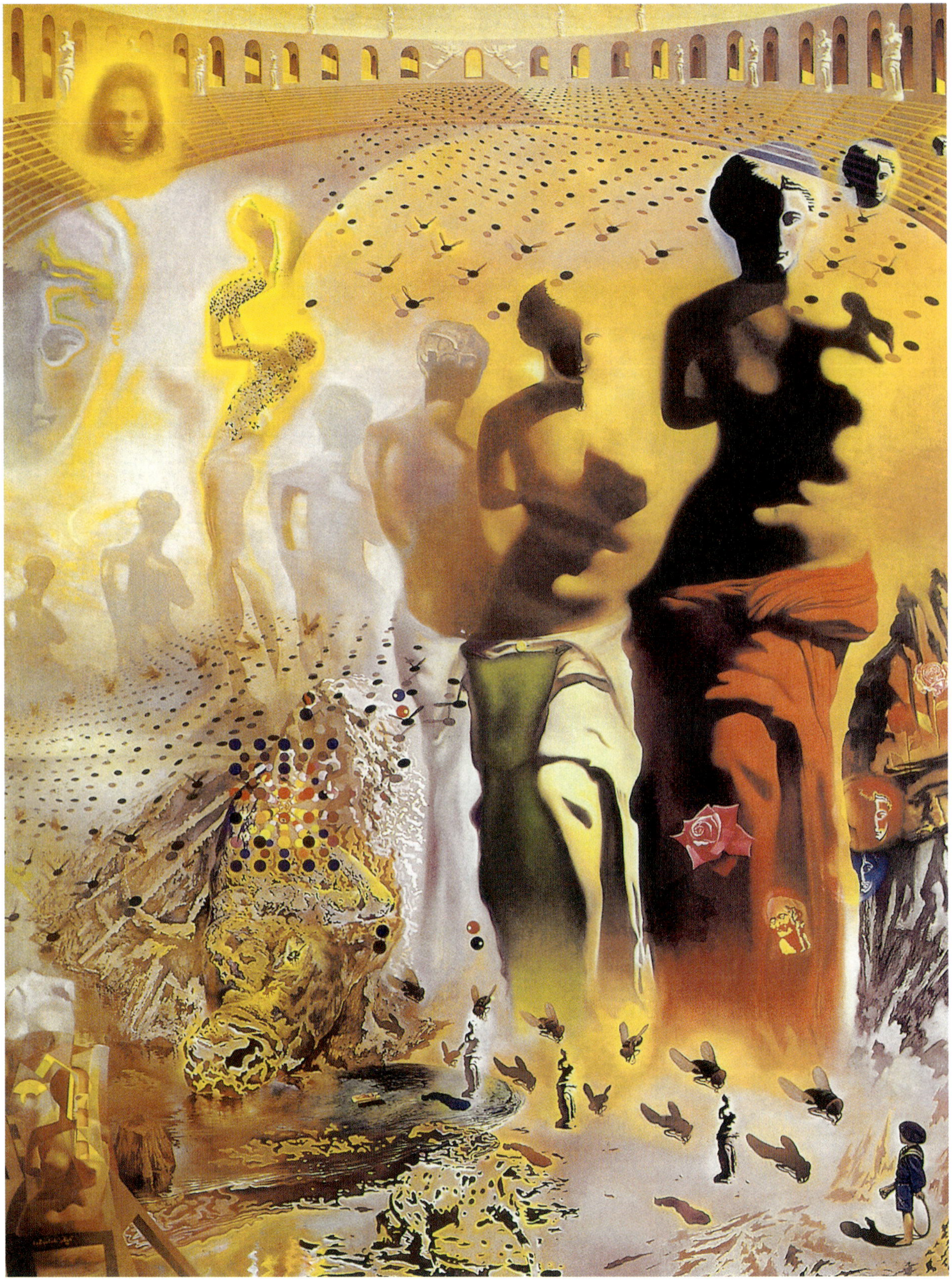

"On the beach of Port Lligat I realized the Catalonian sun [...] to be the thing that had caused the explosion of the atom of the absolute in me. [...] I understood I was destined to become the saviour of modern painting. I became a saint."[39] After Dalí had raised himself to sainthood, he declared Gala Madonna: with glorified countenance she became the "mother of God" in his paintings. In 1949, he painted the first version of *The Madonna of Port Lligat*. As a model for the painting he used Piero della Francesca's *Madonna with Child* from the 15th century. Dalí attempted to demonstrate the dissolution of gravity in this picture. The Madonna is divided into single body parts, which although unconnected are held in balance and in their correct anatomical positions. The Christ child floats in the open belly, which is also perforated. At a private audience with Pope Pius VII in November 1949, Dalí presented the first version of his Madonna. The Pope – as the painter reported, admired the picture greatly. Having reached the pinnacle of his fame, the doors of the mighty now began to open for the Catalonian farmer. And he entered with joy. In 1956, he allowed himself to be received by General Franco, who, eight years later, awarded him the "Cross of Isabel". Critics accused him of allowing himself to be honoured by the murderer of his friends, but he rejected this with the answer: "If I have accepted the Catholic 'Cross of Isabel' from the hands of Franco, it is only because nobody in Soviet-Russia has seen fit to award me the Lenin-Prize. And I would also accept an honour if Mao Tse-tung awarded it to me."[40] Dalí stylized his non-political stand to the point of provocation. He accepted that a group of artists protested against his participation in an international Surrealist exhibition in New York in 1960: each headline increased his popularity and that was good for business. Television, which he described as the "medium of degradation and feeble-mindedness of the masses", was a means for Dalí to become even better known. Spectacular appearances were still more media-effective than provocative declarations, however. On September 3rd, 1951, Dalí and Gala appeared as seven-metre tall giants at a ball in Venice. The costumes were created by the young Parisian fashion designer Christian Dior. In 1955, Dalí transferred his atelier for some days to the rhinoceros enclosure at the zoo in Vincennes, a suburb of Paris, in order to work on his paranoic-critical version of *The Bobbin-Lace Maker* of Vermeer. In the eyes of the art-critics Dalí did not just lose credibility because of his promotion in the media. Since his change towards classicism and Catholicism, his paintings had been more negatively assessed. Despite this criticism, almost all the major museums in the world bought Dalí's works in the fifties. At the beginning of the sixties, Dalí began to make plans for a museum in his home town of Figueras. His choice of building was a town theatre, a classical building from the 19th century, and one which had been very badly damaged during the Civil War.

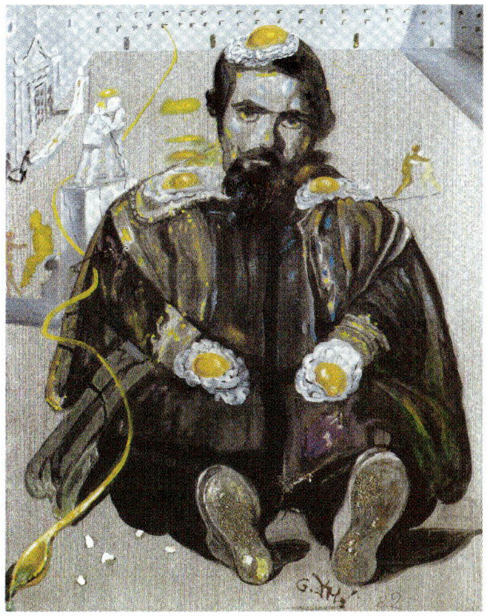

63. ***The Hallucinogenic Toreador***, ca. 1968-1970. Oil on canvas. 398.8 x 299.7 cm. The Salvador Dalí Museum, St Petersburg (FL).

64. ***Velásquez Dying Behind the Window on the Left Side Out of which a Spoon Projects***, 1982. Oil on canvas with collages. 75 x 59.5 cm. The Gala-Salvador Dalí Foundation, Figueras.

At first, Dalí planned to take over the ruins in their damaged state and use them as an exhibition place. In view of the missing roof, however, this proved to be too difficult. Together with the architect Emilio Pérez Piñero, Dalí drafted a dome: "A principle related in particular measure to the monarchy, life and the liturgy."[41] On September 28th, 1974, the seventy-year-old Dalí opened his "Teatro-Museo": it is not just an exhibition place, but also a holy one where the Dalí, the divine, pays homage to himself. He dedicated the dome to Spain's sovereigns – to which the governing dictator Franco also belonged. For Dalí, the time for being honoured began: in 1978, the Spanish royal couple, Juan Carlos and Sofia, visited the "Teatro-Museo". In the same year he was accepted by the French Académie des Beaux-Arts in Paris as an honorary member. The Georges-Pompidou Centre in Paris devoted an extensive retrospective to him in 1979, with over 250 paintings, which was subsequently shown at the Tate Gallery in London. In 1982, the painter was raised to a peerage by King Juan Carlos. And with this, the dream of Dalí's childhood was in one way fulfilled. Fame and wealth marked the last twenty years of Dalí's life. From 1970 onwards, his yearly net income was estimated at half a million dollars. For the administration of his "empire", Dalí employed a small court which almost constantly surrounded him. While in interviews, Dalí always claimed he could never have too much of being in the public eye but Gala wished for a place of peace. In 1967, Dalí bought the half-ruined Château Pubol for Gala, which they renovated and furnished to their own taste. Here was a place to which Gala retreated more and more frequently. The management of Dalí's general affairs, which had been her task earlier, had been taken over in 1962 by John Peter Moore. Moore, a former officer, was replaced in 1976 by Enrique Sabater. Sabater quickly succeeded in becoming a multi-millionaire at Dalí's expense. At the beginning of the eighties, Dalí became ill with Parkinson's Disease. He let himself be treated in Paris, and someone spread the rumor that Gala wanted to separate from him. Furthermore, the psychiatrist Dr. Roumeguère, who had treated Dalí over many years, accused Gala in a newspaper article of tyrannizing and hurting her husband. On June 10th, 1982, Gala died of an infection of the ureter. According to her wish, she was laid to rest at Château Pubol. After the burial, Dalí remained at the château, where he lived a secluded life and carried on working despite his illness. Here, in 1983, he painted his last picture: *The Swallow's Tail* – a cloth featuring geometrical signs, which Dalí borrowed from the formulas of the French mathematician René Thom. The upwardly curving ends of the swallow's tail are reminiscent of Dalí's moustache. A few months after the completion of the painting a fire broke out at the château, the cause of which has never been identified. Dalí survived the fire badly injured. After his convalescence, he returned to his birthplace and lived beside his "Teatro-Museo" until his death on 23rd January, 1989. He was laid to rest there under the dome. He bequeathed his estate – over two-hundred and fifty paintings and two thousand drawings – to the Spanish state in his last will and testament.

65. ***Wind Palace***, 1972. Ceiling painting of the Old Teatro Museo.

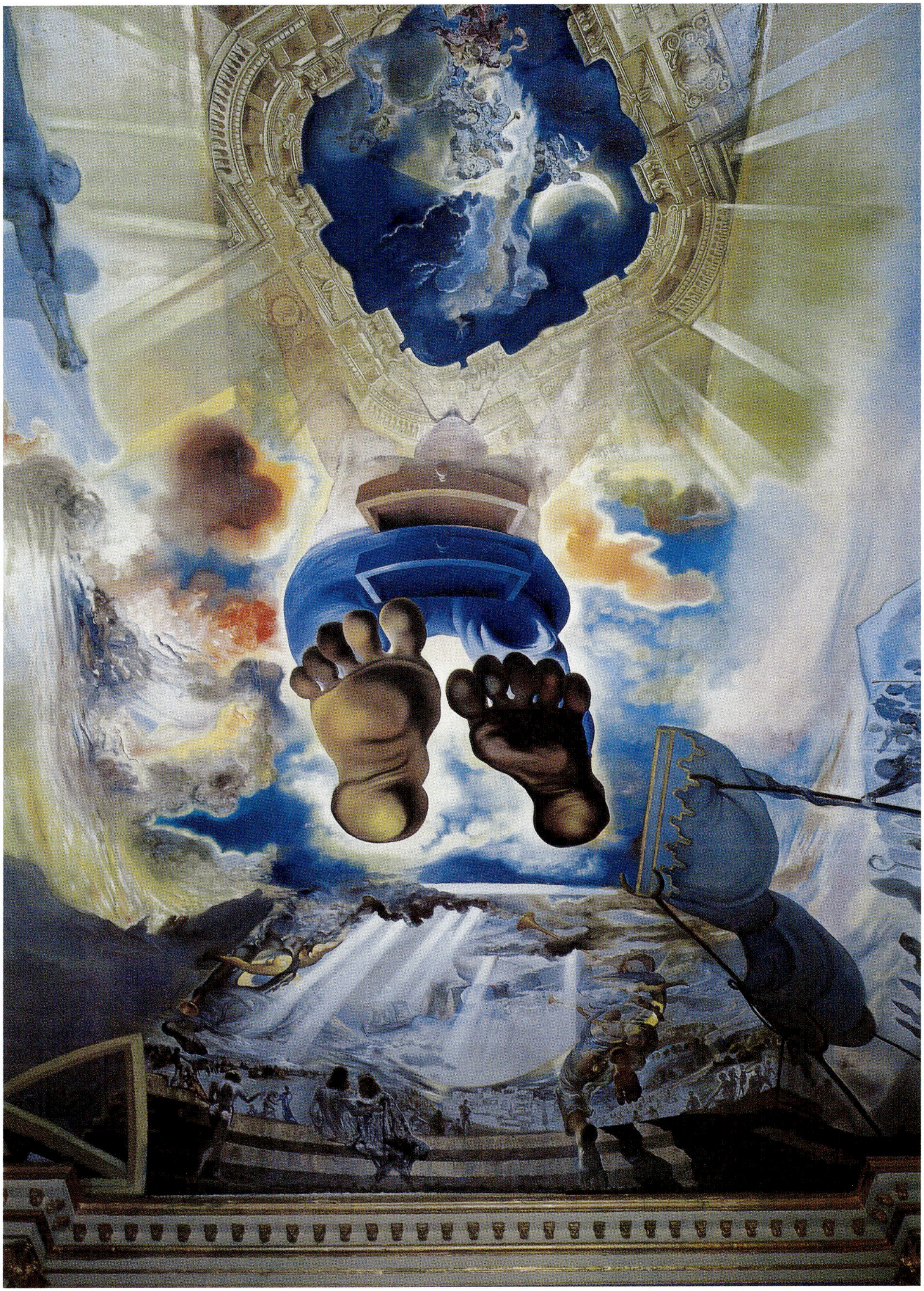

LIST OF ILLUSTRATIONS

NOTES

1 Salvador Dalí, *The Secret Life of Salvador* Dalí, New York, 1942, p. 42.
2 Salvador Dalí, *The Secret Life*, p. 47.
3 Salvador Dalí in a television interview with Pierre Cardinal for French television in 1975.
4 Salvador Dalí, *The Secret Life*, p. 92.
5 Salvador Dalí, *The Secret Life*, p. 92.
6 Television interview from 1975.
7 Salvador Dalí, *The Secret Life*, p. 29.
8 Salvador Dalí, *The Secret Life*, p. 173.
9 Salvador Dalí, *The Secret Life*, p. 187.
10 Catalogue 1994, p. 23.
11 Salvador Dalí, *The Secret Life*, p. 196.
12 Salvador Dalí, *The Secret Life*, p. 254.
13 Bosquet, *Discussions*, p. 26.
14 Federico Garcia Lorca, *Ode to Salvador Dalí*, quote from Catalogue, 1979, p. 36.
15 Garcia Lorca family private archive in Madrid, quote from Catalogue, 1979, p. 36.
16 Bosquet, *Discussions*, p. 25.
17 Salvador Dalí, *The Secret Life*, p. 253.
18 Salvador Dalí, *Becoming the Man*, Paris, 1973, p. 85.
19 Salvador Dalí, *The Secret Life*, p. 307.
20 Salvador Dalí, *The Secret Life*, p. 348.
21 Ramón Gomez de la Serna, *Dalí*, Eltville am Rhein 1981, p. 224.
22 Television interview from 1975.
23 Salvador Dalí, *Becoming the Man, p. 142.*
24 Catalogue 1979, p. 132.
25 Salvador Dalí, *Becoming the Man, p. 194.*
26 Salvador Dalí, *Becoming the Man, p. 140.*
27 Catalogue 1979, p. 131.
28 Television interview from 1975.
29 Salvador Dalí, *The Visible Woman, (la Femme visible)*, quote from catalogue 1979, p. 226.
30 Salvador Dalí, *Becoming the Man, p. 173.*
31 Salvador Dalí, *Becoming the Man, p. 174.*
32 Salvador Dalí, *The Secret Life*, p. 389.
33 Salvador Dalí, *The Secret Life*, p. 415.
34 Salvador Dalí, *The Secret Life*, p. 424.
35 Salvador Dalí, *The Secret Life*, p. 465.
36 Television interview from 1975.
37 Catalogue 1979, p. 348.
38 Salvador Dalí, *Becoming the Man, p. 243.*
39 Salvador Dalí, *Becoming the Man, p. 243.*
40 Bosquet, *Discussions*, p. 4.
41 Ramón Gomez de la Serna, *Dalí*, p. 193.